SOME FEET HAVE NOSES

SOME FEET

Lothrop, Lee & Shepard Books   *New York*

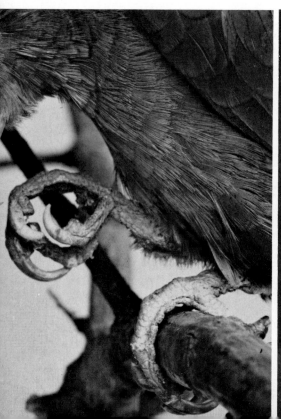

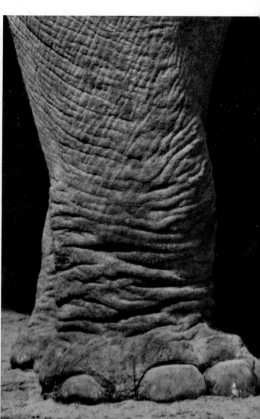

HAVE NOSES
Anita Gustafson
Drawings by APRIL PETERS FLORY

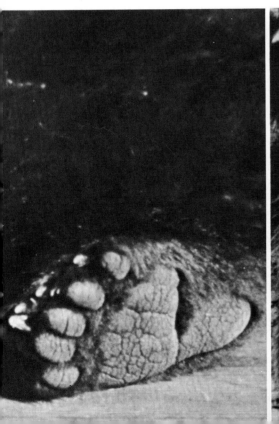

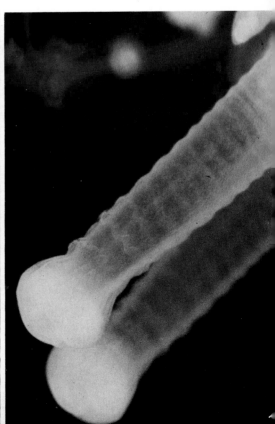

FOR MEG

Who likes shoes and what goes in them

Photographs on pages 2, 3, 6, 16, 26, 28, 32, 34, 35, 49, 50, 55, 57, 58, 65, 66, 67, 82, 85, and 87 courtesy of the American Museum of Natural History; page 11 courtesy of the Bettmann Archive, Inc.; page 12 courtesy of Wide World Photos, Inc.; page 23 by David Schwimmer, Bruce Coleman, Inc.; page 38 by Robert Gossington, Bruce Coleman, Inc.; page 45 by Frank W. Lane, Bruce Coleman, Inc.; page 60 by J. Scott Altenbach; page 68 courtesy of Animals Animals/Leonard Lee Rue III; page 78 by Keith Gunnar, Bruce Coleman, Inc.

ON THE TITLE PAGE: *Top: Hairy Woodpecker. Bottom row: Amazon Parrot, Domestic Feline, Indian Elephant, Black Bear, Tarantula, Common Sea Star*

Library of Congress Cataloging in Publication Data

Gustafson, Anita.
Some feet have noses.

Bibliography: p.
Includes index.
Summary: Discusses the evolution of the foot, an extremely useful but often overlooked appendage.
1. Foot—Juvenile literature. [1. Foot]
I. Flory, April Peters, ill. II. Title.
QL950.7.G87   591.1'042   81-15573
ISBN 0-688-00925-5
ISBN 0-688-00926-3 (lib. bdg.)

CONTENTS

1. A Look at the Foot 7

2. How Many Feet Are Enough? 17

3. The Incredible Starfish Tube-feet Machine 27

4. Feet That Smell 33

5. The Fin-feet 39

6. Talking About Toes 51

7. Of Flat Feet, Tiptoes, and Toenails 61

8. What Good Is a Foot? 69

9. Getting Down to the Bottom of Feet 79

10. Another Look at the Foot 91

Bibliography 94

Index 95

1.
A LOOK AT THE FOOT

Most people never think twice about feet. Unless their shoes pinch or somebody steps on their toes, they simply take their feet for granted.

It's easy to see why. You never miss anything until you lose it, and feet are hard to lose. You never have to remember feet. How many people, for example, worry about going off on a trip without remembering to pack their feet? Hardly any. You can count on the fingers of one hand the number of people who think about feet—because they can count on their feet to be there, right at the end of their legs.

But if people thought more about feet, they'd be glad they had, because feet are fascinating.

This little tree frog need not fear—its suction-cup toes will keep it stuck to its pencil as long as necessary.

7

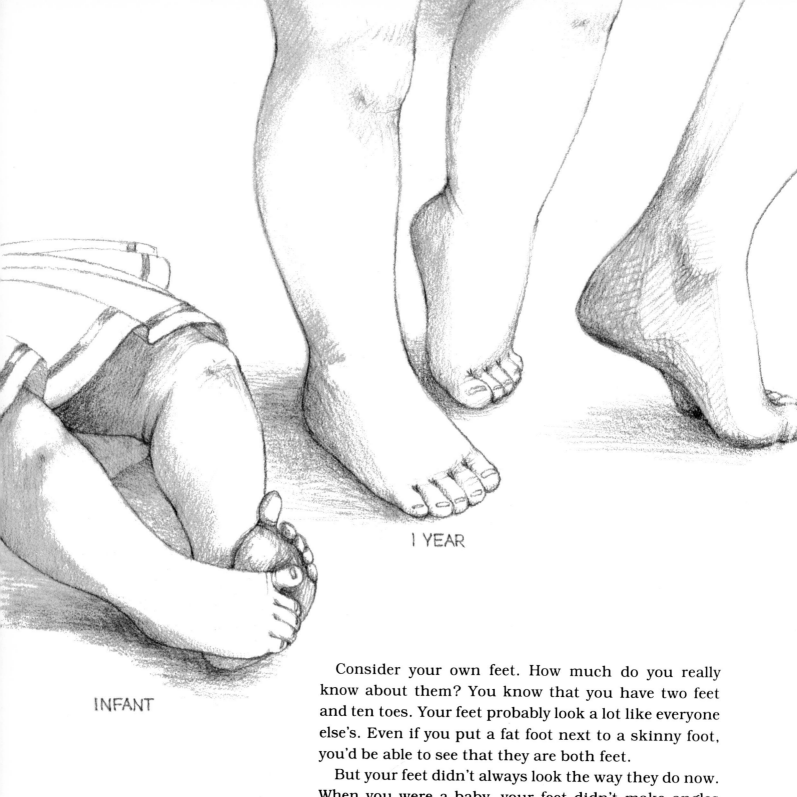

INFANT

I YEAR

Consider your own feet. How much do you really know about them? You know that you have two feet and ten toes. Your feet probably look a lot like everyone else's. Even if you put a fat foot next to a skinny foot, you'd be able to see that they are both feet.

But your feet didn't always look the way they do now. When you were a baby, your feet didn't make angles at your ankles. They were in a straight line with your legs. If someone put their finger under your foot, your foot curled down around it, like a bird curls its toes

SOME FEET HAVE NOSES

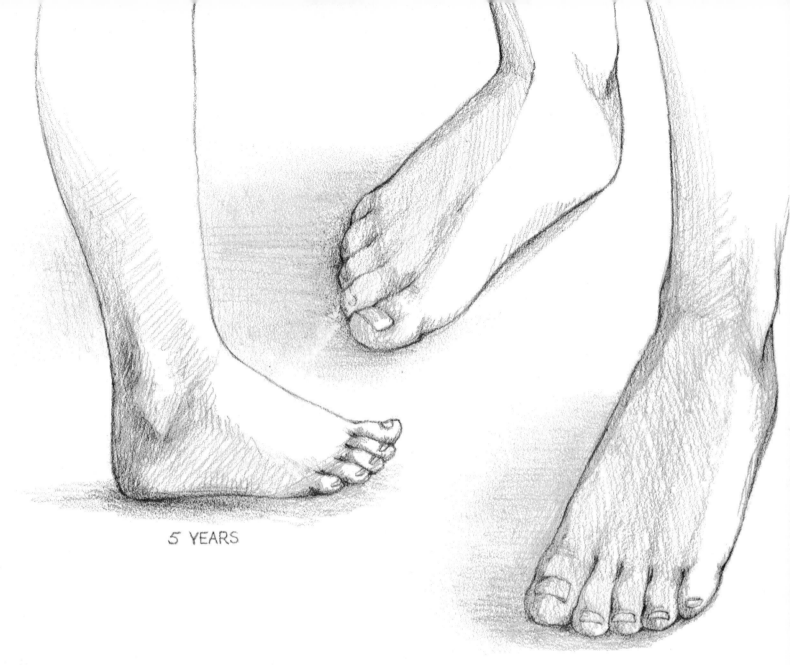

5 YEARS

IO YEARS

down to perch on a branch. Your big toe stuck out like a thumb.

As you grew, however, your feet got down to business. They followed a pattern developed over a long period of time. Without your thinking about it, your feet began to turn at the ankle. Now you'd have something to stand on when you needed it. Your big toes rotated so they were in a line with your other toes. Now, if someone touches your soles, you don't "perch." You may giggle, though, because feet can be ticklish.

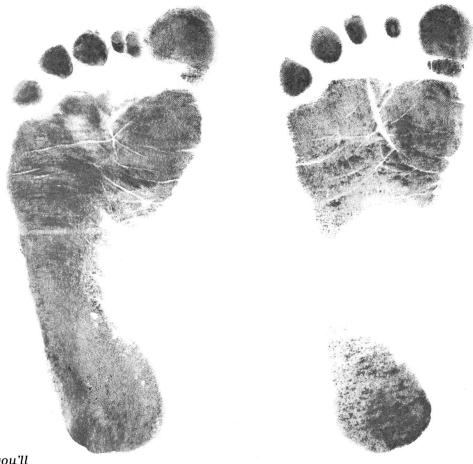

*Look carefully, and you'll
see that even these identical
twins, young Mitch and Ira Rinn,
have non-identical footprints.*

You also know that you use your feet to stand on and to move around on. But did you know that the footprint you leave behind you is as individual and unique as your fingerprint? No other person leaves a footprint exactly like yours.

Newborn babies are footprinted in the hospital. The footprint becomes a permanent part of the baby's medical record and helps grown-ups keep track of which baby belongs where.

SOME FEET HAVE NOSES

The last Empress of China, Tz'u Hsi of the Manchu dynasty. Manchu emperors tried for centuries to discourage foot binding, but it was not until the 20th century that this practice died out.

People of long ago seem to have thought more about feet than we do today. The ancient Greeks thought strong feet were beautiful. They admired the way feet worked as part of the human design. Other people thought feet were beautiful, too, but in a sadly different way.

Until the early 1900s, in China, small feet were the highest mark of a girl's beauty. Some parents bound their daughters' feet when they were little to keep the feet from growing. Binding was painful. You can imagine how uncomfortable you'd be if you were forced to wear the shoes you wore in first grade. But Chinese girls endured the pain because that would save them from being insulted later. To have big feet and be called "demon with large feet" or "goose foot"—terrible! Back then, if a Chinese woman was called "goose foot," she wouldn't show her face in public.

A LOOK AT THE FOOT

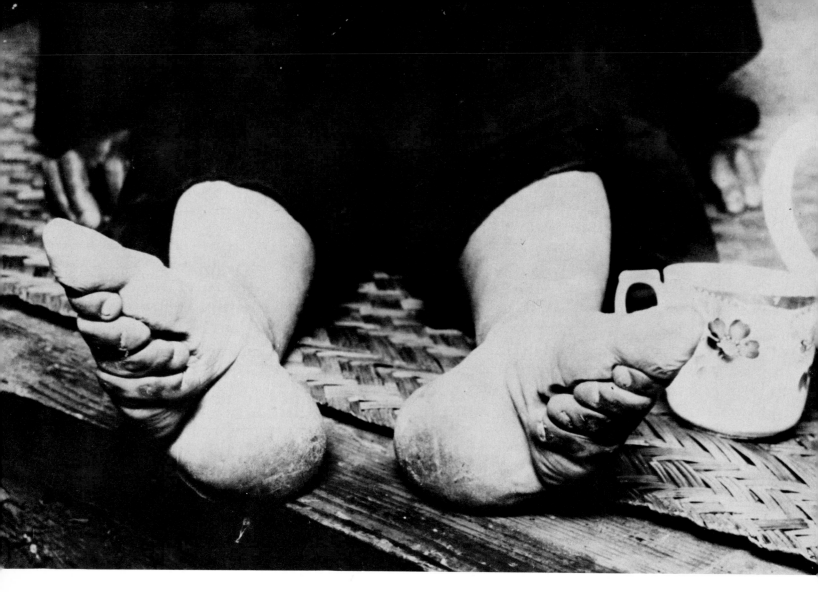

Foot binding was a disfiguring and crippling practice.

When the girls grew up, their tiny feet weren't much good for balancing or walking. They had to move in a smooth series of "bird hops." They found a way to do this gracefully, but they could never again run fast or play hard.

Why were small feet so important if they were basically useless? *Because* they were useless. It was a sign that a girl's parents or husband had so much power and money that she would never have to depend on her own physical strength!

SOME FEET HAVE NOSES

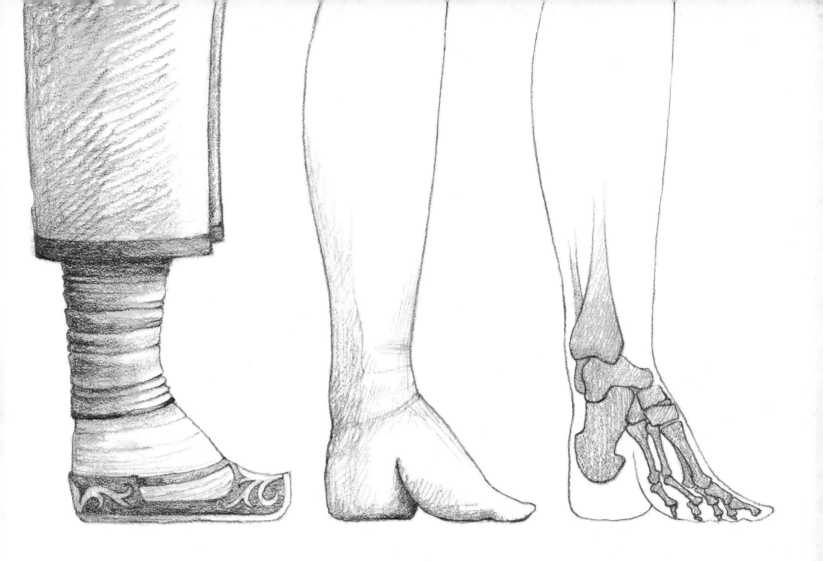

Compare the shape and bone structure of a bound foot, above, with those of a normal foot, below.

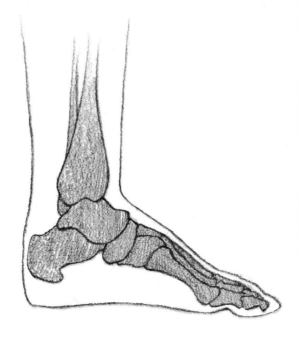

Today the Chinese no longer bind feet. And today, all over the world, people who have unnaturally small feet often have surgery. They go to special doctors called podiatrists. These doctors can lengthen too-short feet in children by lengthening the tendons so the feet are allowed to grow. Podiatrists can help short-footed adults, too, by grafting, or inserting, extra bone. Feet of the right length keep people from falling over all the time.

A LOOK AT THE FOOT

Even if most people don't think about feet today, they talk about them continually. We "land on our feet" when we are lucky. We "put our foot in it" when we make a mistake. We "put our foot down" when we insist on something. When we start something, we "get it on its feet."

We even say how we feel about other people by talking about their feet. We are "on a good footing" with someone when we're friends. We "trample someone underfoot" when we're mean to them. When they're mean to us, they have their "feet on our necks."

Some sayings about feet are firmly rooted in superstition. "Let's get off on the right foot," we say. And the right foot was the *right* foot and not the left one. The

SOME FEET HAVE NOSES

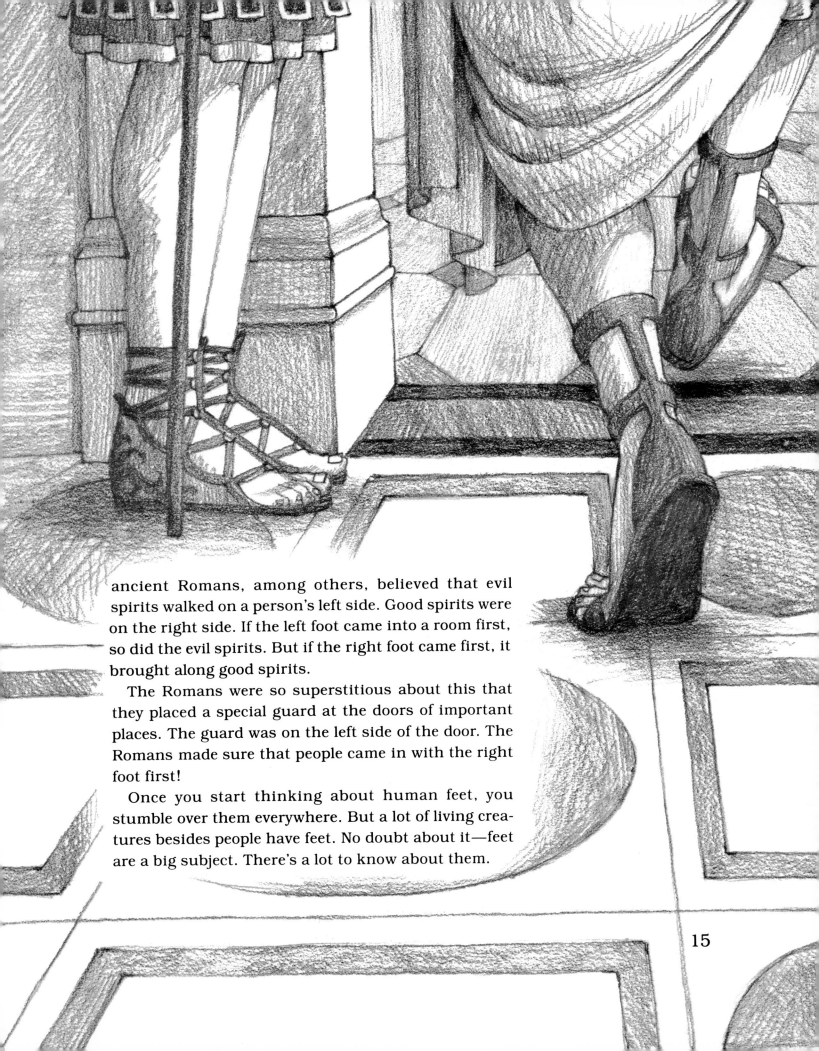

ancient Romans, among others, believed that evil spirits walked on a person's left side. Good spirits were on the right side. If the left foot came into a room first, so did the evil spirits. But if the right foot came first, it brought along good spirits.

The Romans were so superstitious about this that they placed a special guard at the doors of important places. The guard was on the left side of the door. The Romans made sure that people came in with the right foot first!

Once you start thinking about human feet, you stumble over them everywhere. But a lot of living creatures besides people have feet. No doubt about it—feet are a big subject. There's a lot to know about them.

Four feet are not quite enough for this kangaroo, who uses its tail in place of a nonexistent fifth foot, thus freeing up its forefeet for self-defense.

2.
HOW MANY FEET ARE ENOUGH?

One of the first things to know about feet is how many of them are enough. Most vertebrates, or animals with backbones, have two pairs of appendages. We are vertebrates, and one pair of our appendages is specialized into arms and the other into legs, complete with feet. We find that two feet are enough, but other animals have a different number of feet—one or six or eight or five hundred! There are also animals that don't have feet. Some of these animals once did, but they don't now.

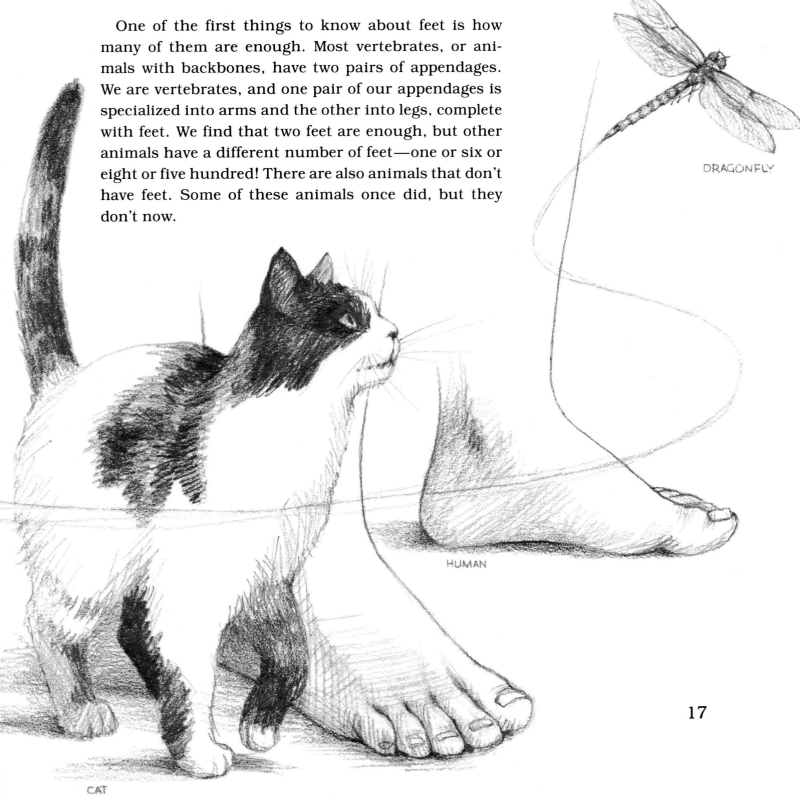

DRAGONFLY

HUMAN

CAT

17

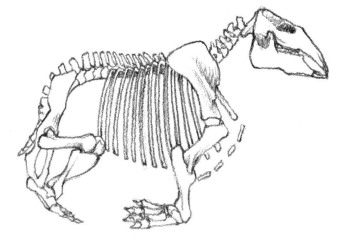

PALEOPARADOXIA

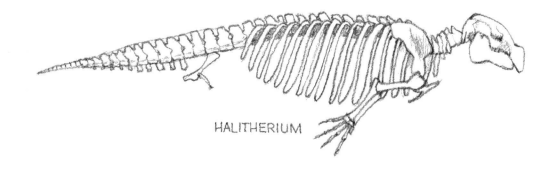

HALITHERIUM

BLUE WHALE

The paleoparadoxia lived about 50 million years ago, the halitherium lived about 35 million years ago, and the blue whale lives today, but each of these water-dwelling mammals evolved from a common stem. As you examine their skeletons, can you see how they adapted to life in the water?

If you asked a mermaid how many feet are enough, she might say, "Who needs feet?" Then, with a flip of her fishlike tail, she'd swim away. True, mermaids are imaginary, but some real-life animals would agree with

SOME FEET HAVE NOSES

her completely. Most snakes and worms would. So would the worm snake, which is neither a worm nor a snake. The worm snake is an amphibian, an animal that can live both on land or in water. It doesn't have legs as most amphibians do. It looks like an earthworm, but, unlike the earthworm, it has a mouth and eyes.

Whales, dolphins, and porpoises have more use for a tail than for feet. These animals once lived on land and probably had decent enough feet, but feet were useless when they went back to the sea. What were once legs and feet changed slowly over thousands of years into flippers. This happened in a process called evolution. Simply put, evolution works like this:

A plant or animal is born and is different from its parents. If that difference helps the young one survive long enough to grow up and produce its own family, the change is a good one. A successful trait has appeared; it may be passed on to later generations.

As time goes on, the world gradually changes. It grows hotter or colder, dryer or wetter. Or it may be that an animal itself begins to exchange the world in which it lives for another, as the whales, dolphins and porpoises exchanged their land world for a watery one. Although all animals once lived in the sea, these particular animals reversed the pattern at a later evolutionary stage. Whether it's changes in the world or exchanges of worlds, new traits now become necessary for survival. Plants and animals can't decide how to change, how to develop new traits. Evolution proceeds slowly and by chance. The final test of a new trait is life. Or death.

The evolution of legs and feet into flippers and flukes in the whales, dolphins, and porpoises was successful. Now they get around by swinging their tail flukes up and down, moving forward as the tail swings up.

But other animals that live in the sea do have feet. Some have only one foot. Clams, oysters, scallops, and other mollusks are all one footed. Together, these animals are classed as Pelecypoda. The name means "hatchet foot."

Take one look at a clam and you'll see that a "hatchet foot" isn't built for speed. A clam has two shells held together on the back with a tough elastic cord, which points up. When a clam is resting, it lies partly buried in mud or sand on the bottom.

When a clam takes a walk, it pushes out its foot, which spreads the hinged shells, or valves. The clam points its foot forward. Inside the foot is a cavity. Colorless blood flows into this cavity and the front of the foot swells up. Now the clam's foot looks like the cutting edge of a hatchet. But the clam's hatchet foot doesn't cut anything. Instead, the hatchet forms an anchor. The muscles of the foot contract, pulling against the anchor as the clam drags itself forward, moving inch by inch through the mud like a living plowshare.

Clams aren't speedy, so we can't say that they eat on the run. They do, however, eat on the creep. They feed on tiny bits of food they strain out of the water as they inch along.

If an enemy seems to be interested in eating them, clams protect themselves with their two heavy shells. They can pull themselves inside, clamp their shells together "tight as a clam," and hide. Most of the time, that's protection enough.

Different kinds of mollusks live in the salty seas, in fresh waters inland, or on land. One mollusk has given its name to the rate at which most mollusks move—a "snail's pace." But speed isn't always important. And one foot is enough for a clam, and for its mollusk relatives.

MUSSELS

QUAHOG

SCALLOPS

MOON SHELL

CHANNELED WHELK

OYSTERS

A sea worm, on the other hand, has evolved differently. The marine worm nereis simply grows as many feet as it has time for.

Look at a nereis and you'll see that its body is ringed, just as an earthworm's body is. Each of the rings is a segment. Each nereis segment, except the head and the last, is exactly alike on the outside. It's almost exactly alike on the inside, too.

On each side of each nereis segment is a foot. The worm's feet don't look much like feet. They are fat, flat lobes. Each lobe has bristles. When the nereis swims, all the little side feet help. They work together like a row of pudgy paddles. But most of the time, the nereis is content to stay in a burrow on the bottom. The bristles on its feet help it hold on to the smooth walls.

When a young nereis hatches from its egg, it has already grown three segments with bristles. Not until after it has hatched does its head grow. Then the little worm settles down to the bottom. It digs a burrow to live in. The nereis will continue to grow as long as it lives, simply by adding on new segments, each with two more side feet. Every new segment develops just in front of the last segment. Along the New England coast, one kind of nereis (*Nereis virens*) can grow to be a foot and a half in length. On Pacific shores, another kind (*Nereis brandti*) can become as broad as a garter snake and three feet long. However, most nereis measure in at less than one inch long.

If you put all the animals in the world on a scale from least to most complex, the nereis would fall right in the middle. If you moved up the scale a bit, you'd run into an animal that looks a lot like the nereis—the centipede.

Both centipede and nereis have long, narrow bodies. Both have many pairs of legs. And the centipede, like the nereis, grows longer as it grows older, adding on

A nereis, or marine clamworm, showing its rows and rows of paddle-like feet.

pairs of legs as it grows. Unlike the nereis, though, the centipede doesn't simply add on another segment. A centipede's skeleton is its skin. In order for a centipede to grow, the skin must be shed. The centipede is not a worm, however much it looks like the worm nereis. Centipedes are one class in the "jointed-legged" group of animals, the arthropods.

HOW MANY FEET ARE ENOUGH?

PINK SHRIMP

NORTHERN
LOBSTER

HERMIT
CRAB

BLUE CRAB

TRAP DOOR
SPIDER

SCORPION

The arthropods of today are the result of 500 million years of changes in the basic body plan of the nereis and other worms. Here segments fused together; there a pair of legs modified and their use specialized. What worked went on; what didn't disappeared. The changes were astonishingly varied.

They were tremendously successful, too. Today, the largest number of species in the world is contained in this group—more than a million! Arthropods eat more of the world's food than other animals do, and they eat more kinds of food than any other group of animals does. There are more arthropods alive than there are any other kind of animal. Seventy-eight percent of all the world's animals are arthropods. (Match that against the number of animals with backbones. Only six percent of the world's animals are vertebrates.) Anywhere you go, you could stumble over an arthropod, because they are also the most widespread of all animals.

Eat a lobster in a restaurant and you're eating an arthropod. Take your dog for a walk in the woods and a tick, an arthropod, might hitchhike along. When you brush down a spider's web, you're destroying the home of an arthropod. Listen to a cricket chirp and hear an arthropod. The world is alive with arthropods—from crustaceans, such as lobsters, to centipedes, to millipedes, to arachnids, such as spiders and ticks, to insects, such as crickets.

All arthropods have their skeletons on the outside of their bodies in the form of shells. They all have jointed legs that work in pairs. And what wonderful variations of legs appear in the arthropods! Some appendages remained legs, but other appendages became jaws and antennae and so on. Even the legs that remained legs evolved so that different pairs on the same individual look different and have different functions.

GRASSHOPPER

GERMAN COCKROACH

CARPENTER ANT

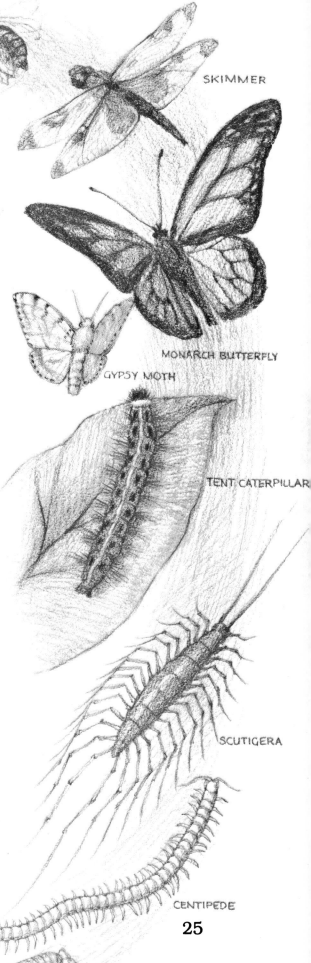

MOSQUITO

HOUSE FLY

CARPENTER BEE

SKIMMER

MONARCH BUTTERFLY

GYPSY MOTH

TENT CATERPILLAR

SCUTIGERA

CENTIPEDE

MILLIPEDE

The legs on the first body segment of the centipede, for example, are poison claws. Curved and hollow, open at the tips, they can inject poison into insects, slugs, and worms. But the legs on the rest of the centipede's body segments are walking legs.

How many feet are enough for a centipede? We call them "hundred-legged worms," but probably the average number of legs per centipede is more like 35 pairs, or 70 legs complete with 70 feet. The only centipedes that may have 100 pairs of legs or more are some that live in the soil. The common species *Geophilus* and *Arenophilus* explore earthworm tunnels for food as far as 30 inches underground. They can grow to a length of almost 2 inches and have 91 pairs of legs—182 feet!

Millipedes, "thousand-legged worms," have two pairs of legs on each segment. But even the longest wouldn't have more than 250 pairs. Still, that *is* 500 feet. . . .

How do they manage to move with so many feet? It's a complicated process. So many pairs of legs and feet must be coordinated. They move in a wave, which starts at the back end. Legs lift, in turn, and swing forward, and then are set down and swung back. The wave is repeated over and over.

There does seem to be a point at which more and more feet get less and less rewarding. The more feet a centipede has, the slower it runs. The soil centipedes, which have the most legs of any centipedes, run more slowly than the ones with fewer pairs of legs. Millipedes run much more slowly still.

More specialized arthropods—arachnids and insects—have fewer feet. Spiders and their fellow arachnids have eight. Insects get by with six.

How many feet are enough? You've seen how many answers to that question appear in the living world. But there is no answer more fascinating than the one found in an animal that is an ancient machine . . . .

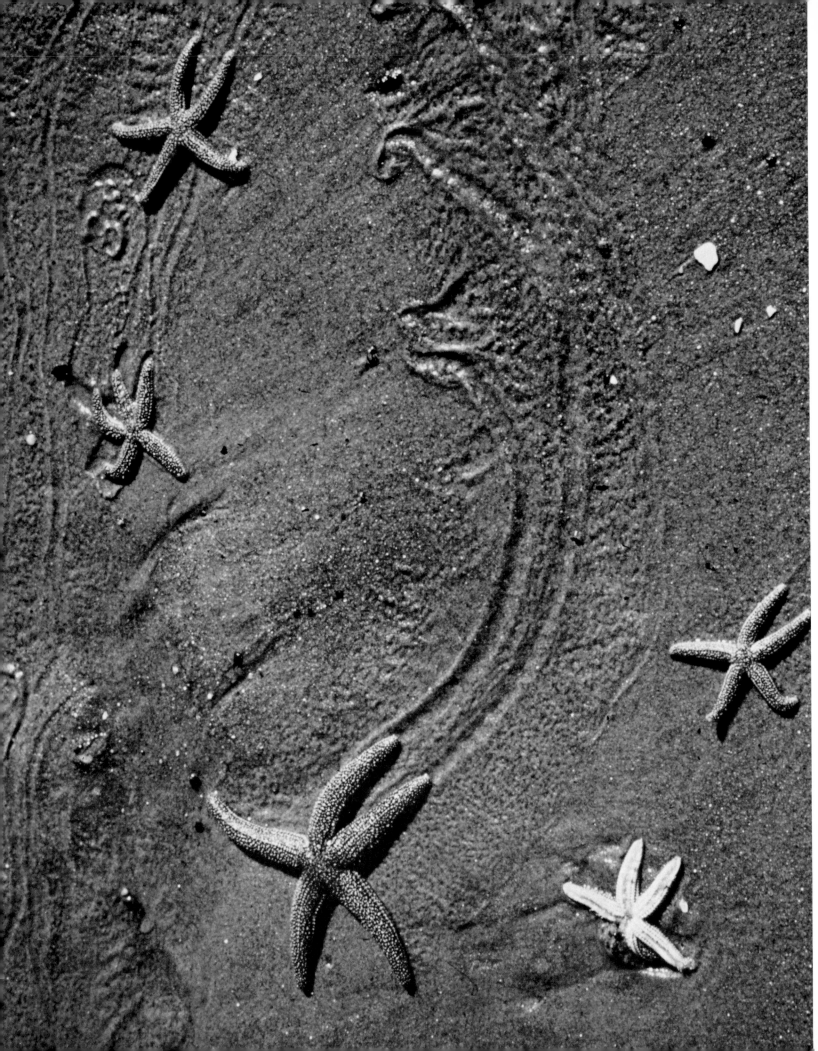

3.
THE INCREDIBLE STARFISH TUBE-FEET MACHINE

For 600 million years, an incredible animal has lived in the seas. During that time, the dinosaurs came and the dinosaurs went. But generations of this animal kept appearing. And still today they are born and survive—these incredible machines, these stars of the seas.

Starfish have found the sea bottom to their liking. Any kind of bottom—mud or sand or rock, along the coast or further out. They are a member of a peculiar group of animals with spiny skins, the echinoderms. All the echinoderms live in the sea. Few can swim and none can fly. The "spiny-skins" don't fit neatly into an evolutionary scheme. As a group, they're just there. They're just something that worked and so . . . they survive.

Sea stars have difficulty moving along on wet sand, but they leave an interesting and pretty trail behind them.

SEA STAR

A close-up view of a common sea star's tube feet.

Starfish come in several sizes and kinds, but even the common sea star is uncommon enough. Those along the Atlantic coast, from Maine to the Gulf, even come in various colors. From purple through bronze, green, orange, or brown, the machine is a marvel, a feat of feet!

The sea star uses its feet to move. But it doesn't move with ropes of muscles and levers of bones. The sea star's feet are hollow tubes. They are thin-walled cylinders

SOME FEET HAVE NOSES

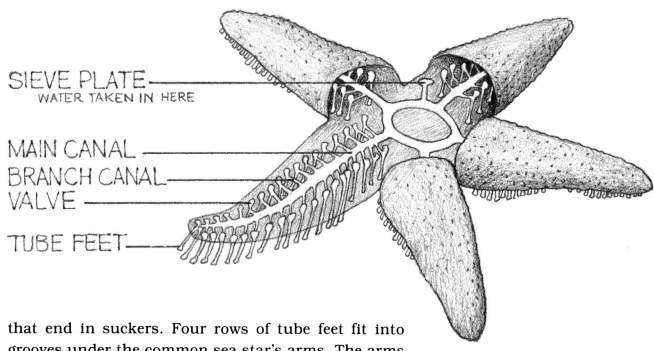

SIEVE PLATE
WATER TAKEN IN HERE

MAIN CANAL
BRANCH CANAL
VALVE

TUBE FEET

that end in suckers. Four rows of tube feet fit into grooves under the common sea star's arms. The arms are not limbs like ours. The sea star's arms are lobes of its body.

Watch it move.

It takes water into openings on its upper surface. The water moves down through the sea star until it reaches canals which run through each arm. From each major canal, the water flows into a tube foot through little branch canals. The water can't back up because the sea star closes a valve on top of each tube foot. The water is forced into the foot. The foot stretches out under the pressure of the water and the sucker on the end sticks onto the sea bottom. Now the sea star uses its weak muscles to pull against the suction. The muscles push the water back through the valve and pull the sea star forward.

Here it comes! (Don't stand back yet—the sea star will take a long time to get to where you are.)

A sea star has hundreds of little tube feet. Each one must be coordinated to work with all the others. Sometimes a tube foot will cling too long and be left behind. But somehow everything gets done and the sea star moves slowly along.

THE INCREDIBLE STARFISH TUBE-FEET MACHINE   29

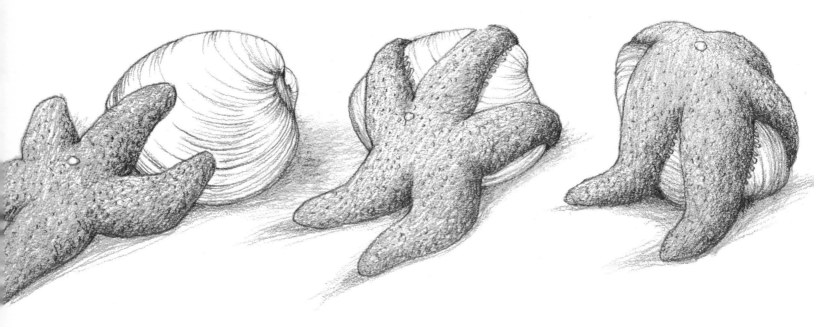

Because moving depends partly on suction, the tube feet can stick only on hard surfaces. When a sea star finds itself in soft sand or mud, it can't use suction. Then the tube feet work like little blunt legs.

The way a sea star moves is incredible enough. But moving is only one part of the tube-feet story. The sea star has another trick up its sleeve. The Incredible Tube-feet Locomotive Machine is also an Incredible Tube-feet Clam Opener.

When a sea star finds a clam, it has found food. The clam hides in its shell—and that's when the sea star goes into clam-opening action.

The sea star places itself opposite the ligament holding the clam's shells together. Two arms go on one shell and three on the other. The little sucker tips are attached firmly. Now the sea star pulls with its muscles, trying to open the shells. The clam is trying just as hard to keep its shells closed. It's a silent, steady war of strain. And in this struggle the sea star has the edge. Usually, the sea star wins.

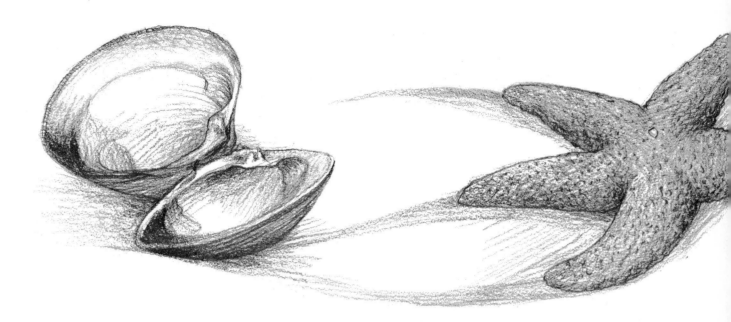

A sea star may be slow, but it is very persistent. This clam never had a chance.

The sea star can use its hundreds of little tube feet in relays, so it doesn't wear itself out. It could tire the clam if it wanted to, but there's really no need to let the war go on that long. With its pulling force of 10 to 15 pounds per square inch, the sea star can actually *bend* the shells of the clam. If an opening of even 1/16 inch is achieved, the sea star can start digesting the clam—while the clam is still inside its own shell!

The sea star can turn its stomach inside out and slide it into the clam's shells. Once the stomach gets through the slit in the clam's shells, glands secrete digestive juices. And now the sea star can relax. Even if the clam clamps its shells together tightly, the stalk of the sea star's stomach won't be hurt. Soon the clam is dead and its shells fall apart. The sea star swallows the clam, swallows its own stomach, and moves off again.

There it goes—the Incredible Starfish Tube-feet Locomotive and Clam-opener Machine, a spiny-skinned survivor from the ancient seas!

4.
FEET THAT SMELL

Meanwhile, back on land, a male spider is looking for a mate. He comes across the scent left by a female. His forelegs move back and forth over the earth. Then, without hesitation, he moves off, following the trail and finding his mate. How can he do this?

Because he is smelling the trail she left behind—*with his feet*!

Spiders have "noses" on their feet. These "noses" don't look like ours, of course. But they are smelling organs, anyway, and they're on the tips of the first pair of walking legs.

A Golden Orb spider attending to its next meal, an unlucky fly.

TARANTULA

The whip scorpion is just one of many arachnids whose feet have "noses"...

Other insects and arachnids have "noses" on their feet, too. Whip scorpions use their first pair of walking legs as "noses." These legs are somewhat longer than the other legs. They are slim and flexible. The whip scorpion uses these legs in much the same way ants use their antennae—to explore what lies before them and to examine things by touching and smelling them.

The senses of taste and smell help each other. You smell with your nose and taste with your tongue. But if you chew a pickle while holding your nose, you probably won't taste much of the pickle. On the other hand, you know how much better freshly baked bread tastes when you breathe in the warm smells as you bite. Sometimes it's hard to know where our sense of smell leaves off and our sense of taste begins.

Taste and smell seem to be closely related in insects as well as in people. Often an insect's senses of taste and smell are lumped together and spoken of as chemical senses.

SOME FEET HAVE NOSES

. . . but this monarch butterfly is no slouch, either, with its feet that "taste."

A butterfly's chemical senses are in its feet. It can and does taste with its forefeet. If a butterfly gets its feet into a drop of water with even a tiny amount of sugar in it, the butterfly knows it has found something good to eat. Immediately, its tongue rolls out and the insect sucks up the food. A butterfly usually carries its long, hollow tongue rolled up neatly below its head, so when it eats, there's no doubt about what it's doing!

Butterflies even use their tasting feet to tell them where to lay their eggs. Many butterflies choose egg-laying sites on plants. After their young hatch, they will be able to eat these plants. The plants become living, growing cupboards. The female butterfly tests the leaves of a plant by "trilling," or drumming her feet on it.

FEET THAT SMELL

Houseflies and bees also taste with their feet. While flies do have other taste hairs around their mouths, they test for taste first by walking all over their food.

Spiders, on the other hand, don't seem to be able to taste with their feet. They can't taste until they actually get their food into their mouths. One spider that lived in a greenhouse caught an ant. He prepared the ant in the usual spiderly way—by injecting digestive juices into the ant to liquify it inside its own shell. But after taking one mouthful, the spider decided this ant wasn't for him. He dashed to a porous clay flowerpot and closed his mouth on it. Soon the awful taste seeped away, absorbed into the pot. Spiders are often sick after eating something they don't like. Life would be easier for spiders if they could taste, as well as smell, with their feet.

The forefeet aren't the only noses and tongues these animals have. They can use their antennae and the palps on their mouthparts as well. But the organs in their feet are very important. A housefly seems to know how important its feet are. It cleans and polishes them regularly by rubbing its legs together vigorously. A housefly, like all the other creatures with feet that smell and feet that taste, takes a lot of care with its feet!

HOUSE FLY'S FOOT

SOME FEET HAVE NOSES

HOUSE FLY

Houseflies depend on their feet for information about food, so they keep their feet in first-class order by cleaning them often.

FEET THAT SMELL

Walking catfish are so successful at life on dry land that they've all but taken over many roads in Florida. Can a fish be a road hog?

5.
THE FIN-FEET

Stepping up the scale from the arthropods, with their skeleton skins, we come to the vertebrates. These are the animals with backbones, the ones that have their skeletons inside their skins.

At one time everything that lived did so in the waters. The only vertebrates were fishes. Some of these ancient fishes had tassel fins. These fins had thick stalks; they were stubby and stiffened with strong bones. Millions of years ago, the tassel-finned fishes lived in lakes and ponds that were not dependable. Sometimes they were filled with water and sometimes they weren't. During the dry times, these fishes faced a difficult situation. They could try to find another lake, or they could stay put and die.

Not surprisingly, the tassel-finned fishes found other lakes. They left their shrinking pools and struggled overland to new ones. They hitched themselves along, inch by inch, on their strong, stubby fins.

If ancient "walking" fishes sound strange, they shouldn't. There are several hundred species of modern fishes that also use their fins to "walk." Some of the fin-feet walk through water over muddy or sandy bottoms. Some move inland and walk along our roads. Some even climb cliffs and trees.

Today's fin-feet come from very different families.

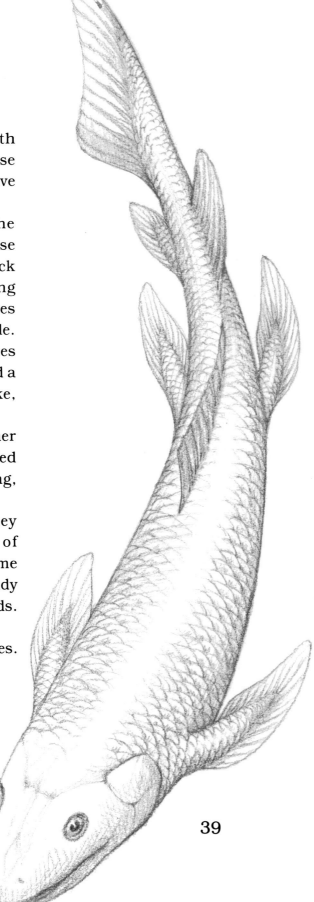

OSTEOLEPIS

39

Probably the ancestors of each species of today's walking fish began to walk independently of each other in the long distant past. Today's walking fish share an evolutionary trait, but they came by it from different routes. So some fishes use one pair of fins to walk and other fishes use another pair.

But tassel fins are where fin feet first appeared. And, in fact, some modern-day fishes have the same kinds of tassel fins that the ancient fishes did. The Australian lungfish, the most primitive of its kind, does. But it doesn't move overland. It uses its paired pectoral, or "chest," fins for resting on the bottoms of rivers as we might use a pair of crutches to prop ourselves up.

A more advanced lungfish, the African lungfish, has whiplike pectoral fins instead of thick-stalked ones. It uses these trim fins to drag itself in a sprawling way along the river bottoms.

In fact, many fish walk through water along the bottom. Skates do. They kick back with their pelvic fins, which are located toward the end of their undersides. Blennies use their pelvic fins to walk, too. Not only can they walk, but they can also climb. One scientist reports seeing some black blennies (*Rupiscartes*) in Samoa that skipped and wriggled up an almost vertical cliff. Other scientists report blennies climbing and crawling over the scientists' own bodies. The fish used their fins almost like little hands.

Some walking fish don't walk overland so much as they "swim" overland. Their swimming movements work both in water and on land. This is the case with walking catfish.

This fish originally came from Thailand in Southeast Asia. Someone in the United States began importing albino walking catfish to sell to aquarium keepers. Several of these catfish somehow were dumped out into the waters in Florida. They flourished. During dry

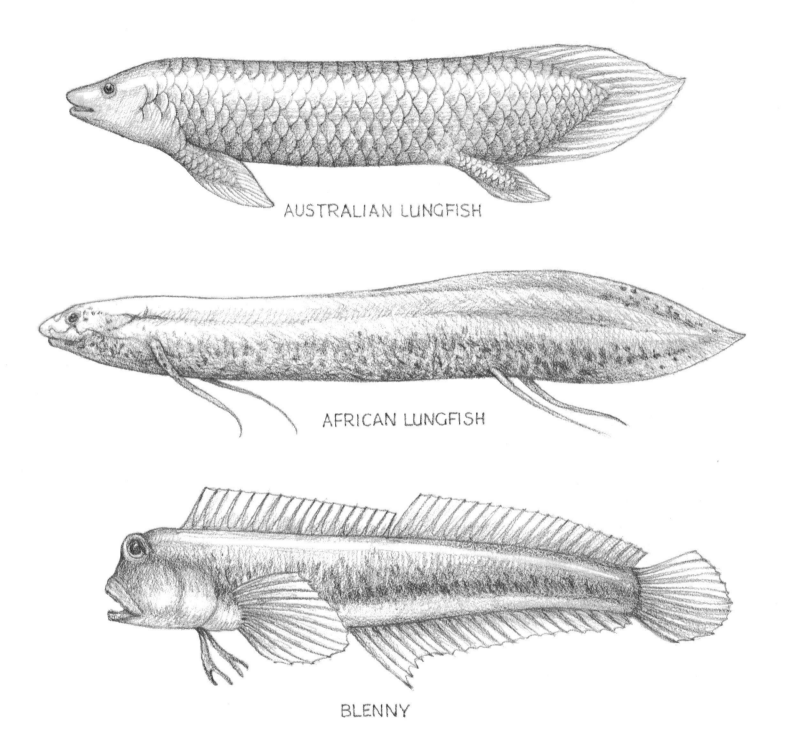

AUSTRALIAN LUNGFISH

AFRICAN LUNGFISH

BLENNY

These lungfish can all get oxygen from air as well as from water, but the blenny can also walk across dry land.

THE FIN-FEET

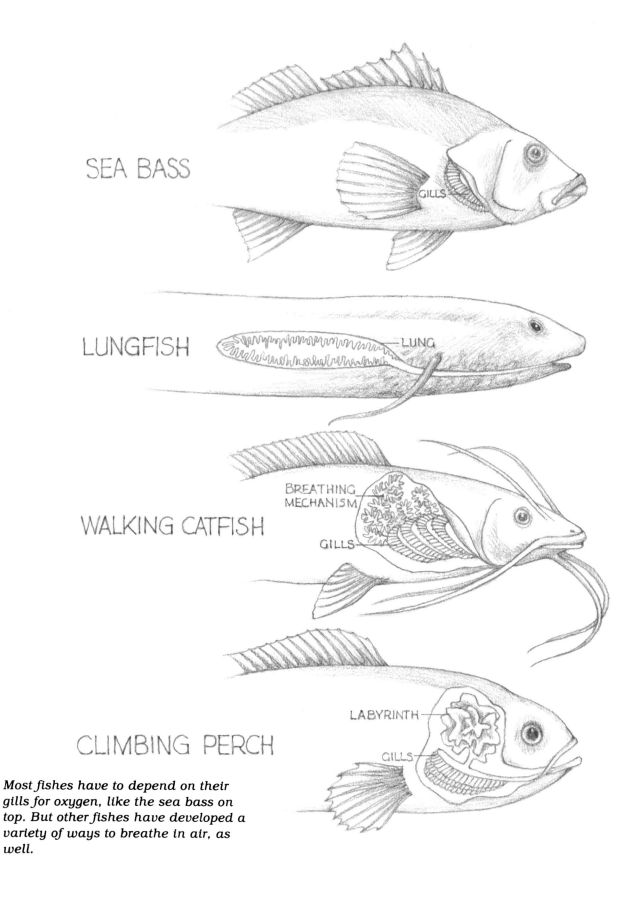

SEA BASS

GILLS

LUNGFISH

LUNG

WALKING CATFISH

BREATHING
MECHANISM

GILLS

CLIMBING PERCH

LABYRINTH

GILLS

Most fishes have to depend on their gills for oxygen, like the sea bass on top. But other fishes have developed a variety of ways to breathe in air, as well.

SOME FEET HAVE NOSES

spells, groups of them leave their watery homes and take a walk . . . along our roads! These hordes of fish are aggressive. They won't be pushed around. Whoever does try to move them off the road will have to deal with what happens if they touch the catfish's sharp poison-tipped spines.

Why do the catfish go for walks? Maybe they go out looking for a new nesting place or for food. Or maybe they just go out for a breath of fresh air—which brings up the question of how fishes breathe.

Most fishes have gills, which take in oxygen dissolved in water. Some of the fin-feet have gills, too, plus alternate arrangements for breathing when out of water and in the open air.

Lungfish, for example, have one lung, which is a modification of the swim bladder, an organ that helps a fish rise or fall to different depths of water. The African lungfish's lung is so well developed that it enables the fish to survive years without being in water at all. During times of drought, the fish makes a clay cocoon with air vents and goes to sleep. You could dig up the cocoon and send it around the world without bothering the fish. When rain softens its cocoon, however, the lungfish inside wakes up, comes out, and goes on with its life. Lungs are the lungfish's method of breathing, either out of the water entirely, or in water so foul that the fish must come to the surface to take in oxygen from the air.

A walking catfish doesn't have lungs. It has gills like most fishes, and uses them when it's in the water. On land, it uses a treelike auxiliary breathing mechanism contained in a pocket above its gill cavities. It's also thought that walking catfish can take in oxygen through their skins.

The climbing perch has still another method of breathing. It has a labyrinth, a system of mazelike folds in a moist pocket above each gill chamber. The labyrinth helps the perch take oxygen from air rather than from water. But even in the water the climbing perch sometimes uses its labyrinth to breathe. It takes in a bubble of air at the water's surface through its mouth and expels the old air from its gill covers.

This perch is a true land walker and not an overland swimmer. Its feet are sharp spines on the lower parts of its gill covers. The perch spreads out its spines alternately and fixes them onto the ground. Then it pushes with its fins and tail. The brownish fish moves over the land with a rocking motion.

The champion fin-feet is the mudskipper. It outdoes the rest of the walking fishes by far. The mudskipper lives in tropical mangrove swamps, where the land and the sea come together. When the tide goes out, this fish doesn't go with it. It isn't held captive by the water's movements, because a mudskipper can get along on land, too.

Mudskippers use their especially strong pectoral fins to prop themselves up in the mud. These fins have an elbowlike base. The fish thrust with their tails. They can hop across the mud flats faster than they can move in the water. In fact, mudskippers can hop faster than most people walk.

But these lively little fish don't have to hop, or skip, to get around on land. They can use their pectoral fins as we use crutches and walk with the aid of their other strong fins, too. Or they can climb trees, using their suckers. The mudskippers are members of the goby family. The whole family has a sucker under the front parts of their bodies. Mudskippers have, in addition, a pair of sucker fins under their walking fins. When they climb, mudskippers plant their body suckers firmly, reach up with the two sucker fins, and up they go. Several little four-inch-long mudskippers may line one

The mudskipper is the champion fin-feet. It can walk, skip, hop, and climb trees and rocks. Who needs water?

THE FIN-FEET

45

mangrove branch during low tide, all of them seeming to be basking in the sun.

The mudskippers' fin feet equip them well to scamper over the mud flats, to inch up trees, or to forage in the mud for something to eat. Their pop-eyes, which can swivel and end with one eye looking up and one looking down, help them spot shellfish or insects or worms.

Mudskippers are hunters. Sometimes they jump at their food with such force that they end up with their noses buried in muck. A mudskipper stalking a snail waits until the snail's foot is fully extended. Then it grabs the snail, rips it out of its shell, and eats it. And that's when the mudskipper runs into a problem.

Out of the water, this fish can't eat and breathe at the same time. The reason for this lies in the mudskipper's unique method of open-air breathing. It doesn't have lung or labyrinth, so people looked for another explanation of how this fish survives out of water. Could the fish breathe in the open air by dangling its tail in water, thus somehow connecting the oxygen-rich water and its own gills? No. The mudskipper doesn't breathe *that* way—but the truth is no less astonishing than that idea.

When the mudskipper leaves the water, it fills its gill chambers as full as it can with a mixture of air and water. The mixture swirls around inside the gill chambers for a few minutes. The mudskipper's gill chambers are folded and have many blood vessels. The water-air mixture keeps the gills moist, and the folds in the chambers take oxygen from the moisture. The mudskipper is like a scuba diver in reverse. Whereas divers breathe air from the surface while they're under water, a mudskipper breathes air from the water while it's above the surface.

The mudskipper's thick skin also helps the fish sur-

THE FIN-FEET

47

MUDSKIPPER

vive in the open air. It prevents water evaporation, so the fish won't dry out.

A mudskipper can live out of water for several days. Or it can live in water. It makes no difference to the mudskipper . . . as long as it doesn't eat. When the fish swallows, the air-water mixture escapes in a rush. The little mudskipping fin-feet must go back to the water to renew its "scuba gear."

Even more surprising than the fishes with fin feet is a curious fin-feet that lives in the desert. Some parts of the Sahara Desert are filled with sand that is "fluid." Just as the sea wind ruffles the oceans, the winds of the desert raise waves in this sand. The tiny grains of sand flow much as water flows. Moving under the dunes of the Sahara is like moving under the waves of the ocean. And a "sand fish" does live and move under the dunes.

The sand fish isn't a fish at all. It's a skink, a common type of lizard. The sand skink "swims" an inch or so beneath the surface. Its wedge-shaped nose and slippery scales help it move through the sand. It moves its body and legs as fish do in water. The legs have spread and the feet have flattened so much that they look more like fins than legs and feet.

Under the sand is a good place for the skink to live. It's protected from the sun's fierce rays. Air trickles

SKINK

SOME FEET HAVE NOSES

The sand skink leaves a distinctive pattern behind as it "swims" under the sand.

through the grains of sand, so the skink can breathe. It eats insects that live in the sand.

It's odd to think of fishes walking at the bottom of the waters and out onto the land. It's even odder to think of a lizard swimming under the sand. Fin feet are useful in the strangest places!

Overleaf: The cormorant's strong, webbed feet make it such an expert diver that the Japanese have used these birds for centuries to catch fish.

THE FIN-FEET

49

6.
TALKING ABOUT TOES

One of the best ways to talk about toes is to talk about birds. Birds' toes are so obvious. With the exception of the snowy owl and the ptarmigans and maybe one or two others, birds' toes are not covered up with feathers. To be totally honest, most birds' feet aren't covered up in any way. What looks like a bird's scaly leg is, in fact, its scaly *foot*. Most of the time, the whole scaly part you can see below the feathers is a bird's foot. Their ankles are where we might expect their knees to be, if we didn't know better.

This explains why some people think that a bird's knees bend the wrong way—to the back instead of to the front. Actually, those people are looking at the bird's ankles and the ankles are bending exactly the way they should.

Once we can look at a bird's claws and think of them as toes instead of feet, we can see that most birds have four toes. The toes may point toward the front or the back, depending on how a bird gets around and finds its food. The toes may be fitted out differently, too, with webs or claws of different shapes and sizes. How the toes look can tell a good deal about how a bird lives.

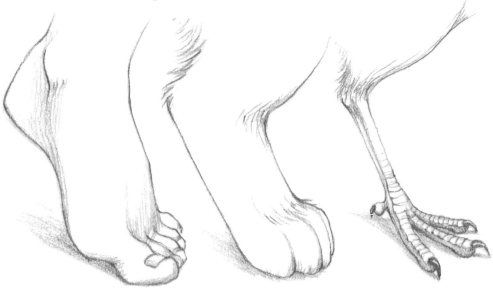

HUMAN   CAT   BIRD

51

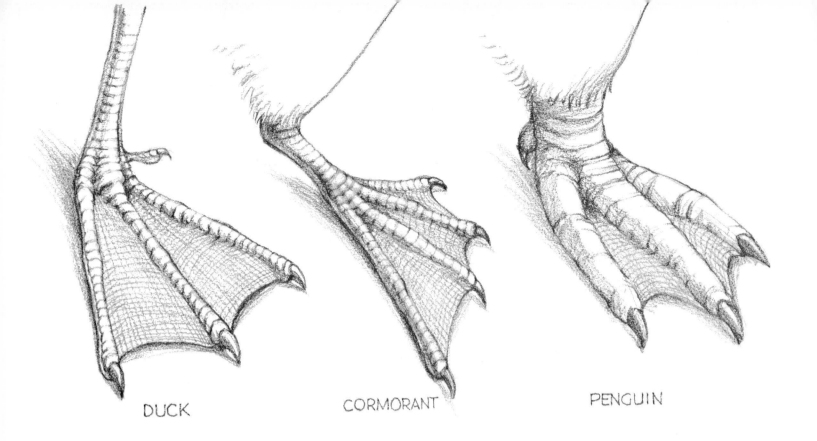

DUCK CORMORANT PENGUIN

Webs between the toes work best for the birds that live on or near water. From the amount of webbing, we can make a good guess about a bird's special abilities. A duck has three toes pointing foward, with a big web between them. Another little toe hooks out, pointing backward. These toes make life as a paddler easily possible.

All of the double-crested cormorant's four toes point forward and have a strong web between them. The extra web surface helps this bird dive and catch fish. Cormorants are such expert divers that the Japanese have used them as living fishing poles for centuries.

The trained cormorants are tied to their handlers by long leashes. One person may handle as many as twelve birds at a time, each on a separate string, without getting the strings tangled. The handlers place rings around the birds' necks. Now the birds can swallow only the smallest of the fish they catch. The rest will stay in their gullets, or throats.

SOME FEET HAVE NOSES

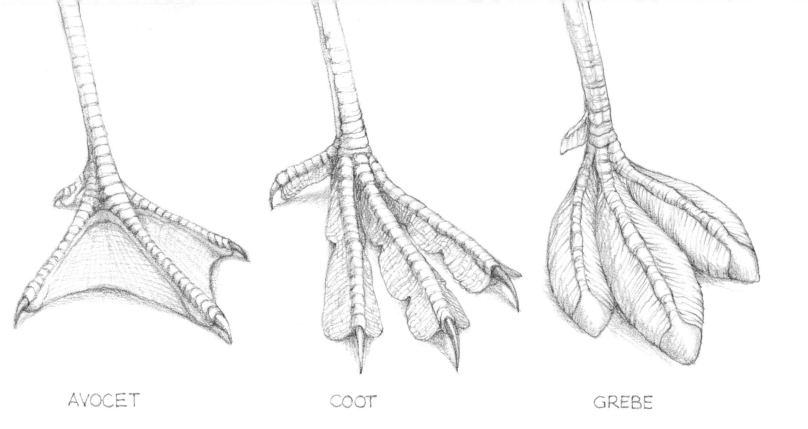

AVOCET   COOT   GREBE

Now handlers and birds are ready to go out in boats. *Ukai*, or cormorant fishing, takes place only on moonless nights. The only light comes from torches the handlers hang from their boats.

The small sputtering pools of light moving over the dark water attract the troutlike *ayu*. The birds dive and easily catch many of them. A handler brings one bird at a time back to his boat and takes its catch. But not all of it—a cormorant is rewarded for its work. The bird gets every fifth fish it captures. Then it goes back to work. When fishing is finished, the birds go home with their handlers. They live in the house as pets.

Another special kind of web is found on the toes of the American coot. These webs are fringes, running along each of the three forward-pointing toes and continuing along the single back-pointing toe. The coot's webs help it swim. They also help the bird walk on the muck and mud around ponds and lakes where it lives. The webs keep the birds from sinking in.

TALKING ABOUT TOES

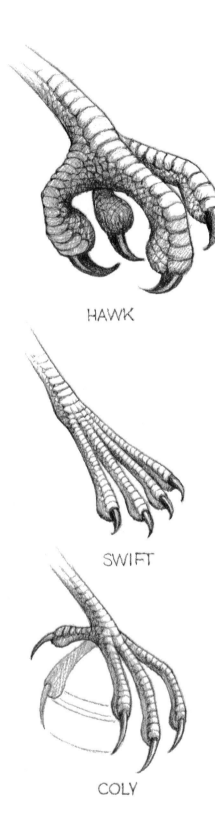

HAWK

SWIFT

COLY

Claws at the ends of curved toes are used for catching hold of and clinging to something. Birds of prey—hawks, eagles, kites, and owls—have two long, strong toes curving forward and two backward. Each of the toes ends with a long, sharp claw called a talon. When these talons catch on to something and the toes pinch together, the birds of prey have a perfect clamp. They swoop down and snatch up a fish or a mouse. No matter how the fish or mouse wriggles, this talon-and-toe clamp is equal to the struggle. Birds of prey seldom drop their food.

Smaller hooked claws on the ends of smaller toes often point to a bird's ability to climb. Chimney swifts have toes and claws they use this way. Their four toes sprawl out forward. The swift can dig its claws in and hang on to the sides of the chimney where it nests. Once the chimney swifts made their nests in hollow trees. Their claws worked well there, too. Many of the small birds that still nest in hollow trees, such as woodpeckers, have curved hooks on their toes to help them climb and hang on.

One of the climbing-clawed birds, the coly, happily spends its time climbing and creeping around in the branches of trees. The coly is also called mousebird, because its feathers look like the soft fur of mice. Its tail is twice as long as its body, so most of the coly's one-foot-long length is tail. All four of the coly's toes point forward, which isn't unusual for a climbing bird. What *is* unusual is that the coly has a swivel toe. The outer toe on each foot can be turned to point backward. With the help of its swivel toe, the coly can climb up or down or simply hang from a branch while it eats some fruit.

Like all birds of prey, this red-shouldered hawk can grasp its prey—or a perch—with its strong talons.

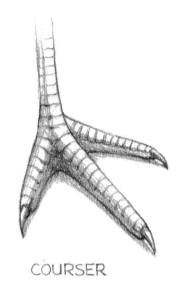

COURSER

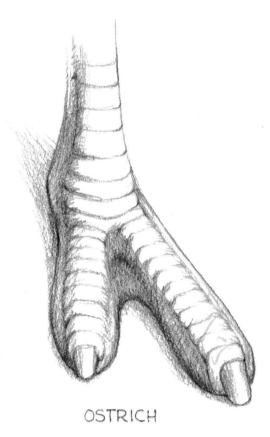

OSTRICH

Running uses fewer muscles than flying does. It costs a bird less energy. And, it seems, running takes fewer toes. Many running birds have lost one or more toes.

The cream-colored courser is a running bird that lives in the desert. It has only three toes, spread wide apart to give it a good supporting surface when it runs over shifting sand. These birds have been called the gazelles of birds because they are so swift and graceful on the ground. They run faster than we walk.

The courser can also fly well, using its short wings. But, oddly enough, the bird flies only when it has to. It prefers to crouch down and blend its creamy color into the surrounding sand. In the face of danger, it would rather hide than fly.

Running is the best way for the courser to find its food. It eats insects that live under stones and sand. It couldn't find them if it flew in the air. So the courser uses its long toes to dart thirty feet this way, then stop suddenly and listen. If nothing moves under the sand, the courser darts sixty feet that way, and again stops suddenly and listens. If an insect moves, the courser hears it and darts its sickle-shaped beak into the sand. More often than not, it comes out with a bite to eat.

Even though it would rather run than fly, there must still be something in a cream-colored courser that wants a "bird's-eye view." Coursers have a peculiar habit of stretching their necks up and peering intently at the horizon. Are they looking for shade from the hot desert sun? Are they looking for danger? Keeping an eye on a good place to hide? Maybe they're just looking in a general way, to see whatever there is to see. Whatever the reason, they stand up on their tiptoes and stare.

An ostrich is always on its tiptoes, not just when it wants to take a look around. It never uses its wings to

SOME FEET HAVE NOSES

fly, but it's the fastest of all the running birds. It can run at 30 miles per hour for 20 minutes without getting tired. One ostrich ran for half a mile beside a car going 45 miles per hour. This ostrich did get tired—not of running, but of having the car beside it. So the bird sprinted on ahead—at around 55 miles per hour—then ran in front of the car and off by itself. This kind of speed from a bird that can stand 8 feet tall and weigh 350 pounds is astonishing. How can it move that fast?

The ostrich's long feet and legs are part of the reason for its speed. And its toes help, too. The ostrich has only two toes—one strong, thick one, with a smaller toe on the outer side. Instead of using the "soles" of its toes as most other birds do, the ostrich uses only its tiptoes. When you sprint, you rise to run on your toes, too. Like the ostrich, you can run faster that way.

A South African ostrich demonstrates its powerful tiptoe running gait.

7.
OF FLAT FEET, TIPTOES, AND TOENAILS

Long, long ago, the ancestors of the mammals first crawled out of the water. They didn't move gracefully because their front and back limbs were short and spread apart. Their bellies scraped the ground. Let's face it—the ancestors of the mammals were awkward.

Today, being awkward is more a nuisance than a danger. Usually, if you're awkward you bump into tables and drop your lunch money all the time. But back then, if you were awkward, you were in danger. You were apt to bump into a predator and find that *you* were being seen as *its* lunch!

As time went on and generations of mammals were born, thousands and thousands of changes took place. Mammals didn't change from what they were basically—warm-blooded animals with some kind of hairy coat and glands to feed their babies milk. As a group, mammals still are essentially like that. But other features changed. And one of the most changeable features of mammals was feet. As a group, mammals display a dazzling array of different kinds of feet.

ELEPHANT

SQUIRREL

All of the feet developed from the fundamental model foot—one with five toes, or digits. The basic posture of this foot is flat. The whole sole of the foot, from toe to heel, rests on the ground. Animals with flat feet walk on the soles of their feet, sometimes using the palms of their hands as well. These animals, the flat-feet, are called plantigrade. We are plantigrades, and so are bears, monkeys, and apes.

Plantigrades are walkers. But they can run, too. The first thing plantigrades do when they begin to run is to raise themselves up so that they are touching the ground with only their tiptoes. They can get a greater push that way—and the greater the push, the greater the speed. Moving on tiptoes is quicker and quieter than slapping along on flat feet.

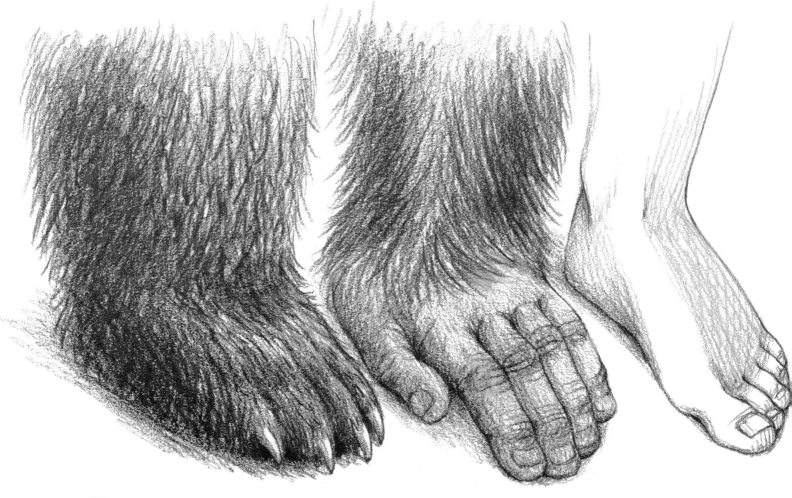

62

BEAR   CHIMPANZEE   HUMAN

So it's not surprising that animals that depended on being quick and quiet to hunt their food evolved into animals that stood on their tiptoes *all* the time. Over thousands of years, the heels and wrists of these animals moved up above their toes. Cats and dogs move on their tiptoes, the tips of their digits. They are called digitigrade animals.

As the dogs and cats became digitigrade, the bones of their feet grew longer. One of their toes no longer rested on the ground. In dogs, this toe got smaller and smaller and stayed with the elevated heel. Now, what used to be a dog's fifth toe is called a dewclaw. The front legs of cats have dewclaws, but every trace of the fifth toe on their back legs has disappeared.

Becoming digitigrade helped hunting cats and dogs run faster than before. The animals they hunted now needed to run faster, too. Speed developed in these animal in several different ways. Some, such as kangaroos, kangaroo rats, and rabbits, became jumpers. Their hind legs and feet grew longer and became catapults. Whatever jumps up has to come down, and the hind legs of the jumpers not only help them jump, but also help absorb landing shock. Other animals evolved into running digitigrades just like their predators. And still other running prey began to move on their toenails.

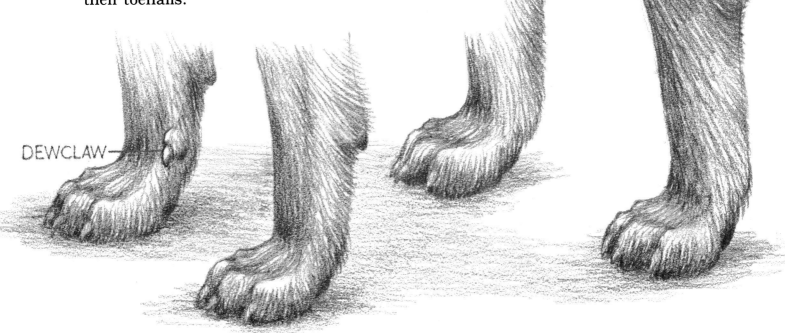

DEWCLAW

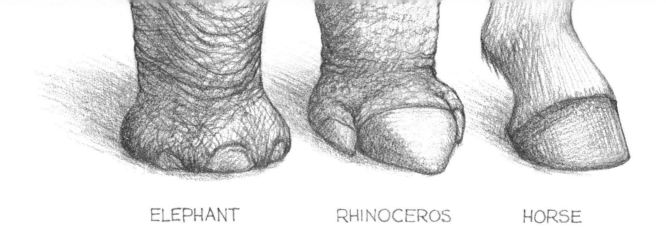

ELEPHANT   RHINOCEROS   HORSE

All animals that run or walk on their toenails are called ungulates. Horses, with a single toenail at the end of each leg, are ungulates. So are animals with cloven hooves, which move on the nails of two toes instead of one.

Ungulate feet, whether single or cloven hoofed, evolved from the five-toed foot. You can still see this basic-model foot today by looking at the end of any elephant's leg. The big toe is the middle toe on the elephant's foot, and it has a strong nail. An elephant is simply so large that it doesn't have to hurry to get out of a hunter's way, so its feet stayed the way they were, and the animal moves by striding.

We can trace the development of hooves in a general way by looking at the feet of familiar animals. Somewhere along the line two toes disappeared from the rhinoceros' foot, but the big middle toe remained and it began to carry more of the rhino's great weight. The other two toes grew smaller. They now no longer touch the ground. The rhinoceros' speed increased when the toes were eliminated. It can move faster than an elephant can. A horse can move much more swiftly still. While the rhinoceros continued to move on flat feet, the horse actually began moving around on a single toenail—its hoof.

HIPPOPOTAMUS   PIG   GIRAFFE

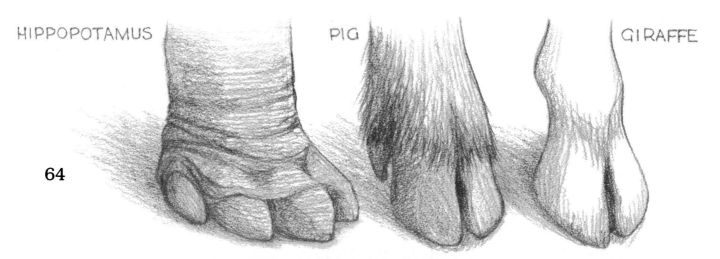

The hippo's four toes spread to make a firm foundation to support its great weight.

Somewhere along the line, the hippopotamus foot lost a toe, too. But only one was lost while four stubby toes remained. This development continued in pigs. The two middle toes of pigs grew large so that pigs walked on those two toenails. Their two outer toes were "leftovers," and, like the dewclaws of dogs, they moved farther up the leg until they no longer touched the ground. The same thing happened with goats and sheep. When the number of giraffe toes dropped down to two, giraffes didn't even keep the other two toes as dewclaws. There is no trace of the lost toes in this animal.

OF FLAT FEET, TIPTOES, AND TOENAILS

Moles are splendidly adapted for life under- ground, with their efficient earth-mover feet.

Why don't all dewclaws simply disappear? Because even though these digits don't touch level ground, they come in handy on other terrain. Deer like to browse in marshy areas. Their dewclaws are useful in keeping them from sinking in and getting mired down. Mountain goats use their dewclaws to keep from skidding out of control when they go down a rock chute. And mountain sheep spread their legs and place their hooves and dewclaws down at the same time when they walk over crusted snow. Walking like this distributes their weight over a larger surface and they aren't so apt to crash through and get stuck in the deep snow.

Mammals have feet adapted to walking and striding, to running and jumping. All of these changes came about because the animals in which they appeared gained speed. They survived to pass the trait on. Running away from, or running after, one another was important to both hunted and hunter. The feet of other mammals adapted to outfit them for special living places. Again, the survival of individuals with these traits passed the traits along to later generations.

Some mammals lived under the ground instead of atop it. Their limbs became good burrowing tools. Moles developed long claws on their five digits to help them dig. Their feet are broad and hairless, and the moles use them to push earth aside.

SOME FEET HAVE NOSES

Squirrels found safety in the treetops. They travel faster going up—and down—than they do over flat ground. In fact, a squirrel can even run along a limb upside down better than it can run right side up over land. Their fingers and toes grew long. Their feet and hands grew narrow. Claws on the ends of their toes now help them cling to trees.

Bats took to the air. They are the only mammals that fly. The membrane that enables them to fly is simply a fold of skin. Some bats have membranes that extend between their hind legs from ankle to ankle. These bats have feet that help them fly. Bats also use their feet as "bat hangers." They hang themselves upside down from their grasping feet, collapse their arms and fold themselves in, and snooze in a cave or some other quiet, dark place.

The lives of other mammals changed even more dramatically than the burrowing mole, the climbing squirrel, and the flying bat. Remember the whales, dolphins, and porpoises that have no use for feet at all? They are mammals, too—at home in the waters.

Porpoises and other cetaceans have no hind feet whatsoever. Their streamlined shapes and skillful swimming make them ideally suited for underwater life.

8.
WHAT GOOD IS A FOOT?

Feet are good for clinging and grasping, for moving from here to there. Some feet are good for smelling and tasting. And at least one tree-living salamander (*Aneides lugubris*) has feet that are good for something startling. These salamanders have no lungs, so they use their feet for breathing! Large blood-filled cavities on the tips of the toes allow these salamanders to breathe in the treetops as the gills of fishes enable them to breathe underwater.

Feet are useful in other, equally startling ways, too. Many animals use their feet as tools. The water boatman is an insect that lives underwater. Its front feet have become "spoons." The "spoons" scoop up algae so the insect can eat. The back legs of the water boatman are broad and fringed with hairs. They have become "oars" to help the insect move around in the water.

Any insect's legs are built along the same fundamental pattern as another's are. But the legs, along with their feet or tarsus area, have become specialized into many different forms. In fact, different pairs of legs on the same insect may be different kinds of tools.

This great white heron is using its toe comb as a tool for cleaning and grooming—or maybe just for scratching an itch.

WATER BOATMAN

69

ARUM FROG   SHEEP FROG

A spadefoot toad has shovels on its hind feet. The spades are horny projections, and they work well in loose soil or sand. The toads dig in their rear ends first. They actually sink backward out of sight, sometimes burrowing two or more feet down. Sinking out of sight is a fine way to escape danger. It's also a good way to keep cool. During dry times, toads may dig in and stay underground for months. They come out when the surface is damp again.

The sheep frog carries an interesting variation on the spadefoot's shovels. This frog's shovels are on the inner edges of its big toes. This little frog—only 1¾ inches long—can bleat like a sheep. If you hear a sheep sometime in Texas or Mexico, you might be hearing a frog!

What else can you use a foot for? A group of professional athletes in Thailand have found another use for their feet. Like Mohammed Ali, these athletes are boxers. Unlike Ali, these athletes box with their feet. Thai foot-boxing is a martial art, like karate and kung fu. Experts in tai kwan do, another martial art from Korea, say they spend around three fourths of their

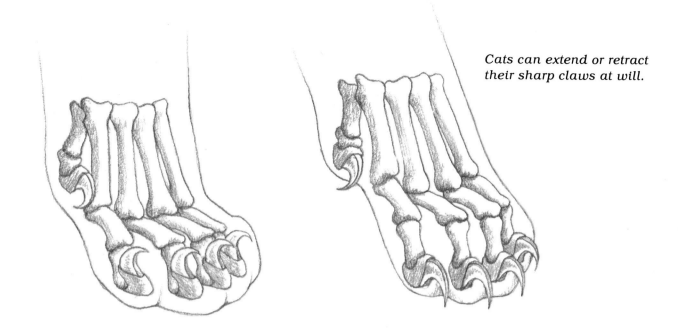

Cats can extend or retract their sharp claws at will.

training time learning how to kick. Feet can be weapons when a person is trained to use them that way.

Many animals use their feet as weapons, too. The only difference is that animals don't have to train. They naturally use their feet. Cats own the finest attack claws. They withdraw their claws into sheaths to keep them protected so they'll stay razor-sharp. Kangaroos may punch a little with their forelegs, but a single wallop from a well-directed hind foot could keep you dizzy for days. So could a blow from an ostrich's foot. Horses can kick with either hind foot or with both at the same time.

Occasionally the weapons on an animal's feet have led to the breeding and training of the animals to fight with each other. Roosters have spurs on the backs of their feet. Cockfighting is an ancient—and bloody—spectator sport. Two roosters are put into a ring and rip each other apart for the amusement of their owners. It's possible that the roosters themselves enjoy this, but the "sport" itself is outlawed in many places.

WHAT GOOD IS A FOOT?   73

Some animals use their feet as we use our hands—to hold on to objects and move them around. Raccoons, squirrels, and kangaroos all use their forefeet as hands. The forelimbs of these animals are almost like our arms.

But the arms of parrots are wings. So parrots use their feet to grasp and hold and move objects. So do all the parrot's family—macaws, parakeets, and cockatoos of more than 300 species. These birds are some of the most colorful of all birds. And they are some of the most unusual.

When most birds have lunch, they don't stop. Instead, they fly or hop or paddle around looking for food. But a parrot, and its kin, can lunch in leisure. They eat fruits and seeds. A parrot can husk and hold seeds between its two forward-pointing and two backward-pointing clawed toes. It can hold fruit in one foot, stand on the other, and bite off whatever it wants to eat. No other birds can do this.

A hand is a good thing to have. Two hands are better. One of the biggest reasons hands are terrific for people is that we have a thumb that can press against our other fingers—an opposable thumb. With this opposable thumb we can pick up and handle most of the things we need to pick up and handle. People have gotten accustomed to using hands to do these things and letting their feet move them around.

Parrots can perch and eat at the same time, thanks to their grasping feet.

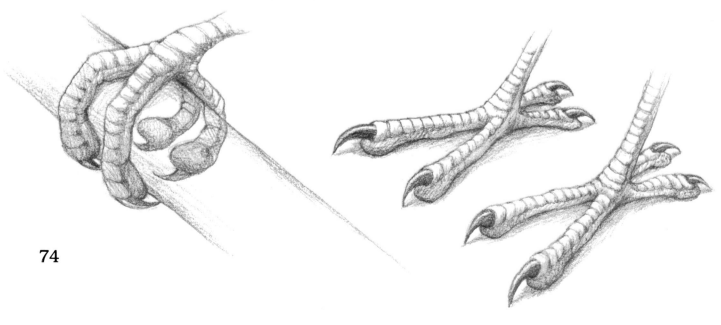

PARROT

MACAW

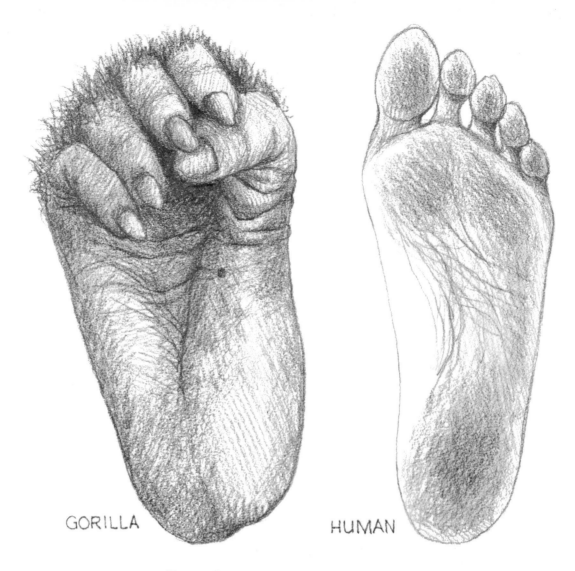

GORILLA   HUMAN

But other primates—monkeys and apes—never developed as great a degree of hand/foot division of labor as people did. With the exception of gorillas, monkeys and apes have longer arms and legs, toes and fingers than we do. They have opposable thumbs and opposable big toes. While we can turn our hands palm down or cup our hands palm up, our feet usually stay planted sole down. But monkeys and apes can cup their feet, too.

When a monkey flies free in the tops of the trees, chattering and playing and using its hands and its hand-feet, what person doesn't envy it? A hand *is* a good thing to have. Maybe four hands would be even better than two!

          SOME FEET HAVE NOSES

TENT CATERPILLAR

For many animals the good of a foot is something other than tool or weapon or hand. Putting their feet down makes most animals feel good. When their feet are where they're supposed to be, the whole animal feels secure and safe.

If you hold a caterpillar on a leafy twig out of a fiftieth floor window overlooking a busy street, the caterpillar won't be bothered . . . if its crochet-hook feet can feel a leaf. But take the caterpillar back inside, set it down safely, and take its leafy twig away, and the caterpillar will panic. It will twist and turn and won't feel right until its feet feel the leaf under them once again.

Centipedes also get a feeling of security when their feet are firmly planted. Put a centipede into a big glass jar on a well-lighted table. The centipede will hate it. But if you put a clear glass rod next to the centipede, it will start to calm down. It will run into the glass rod and be quiet as soon as its feet can touch the sides of the rod. Centipedes hate the light, but they hate not having their feet braced even more.

Salamanders and other amphibians show the same behavior. So long as their feet are touching the walls, everything is all right. As a matter of fact, most animals feel better when their feet are touching their own kind of ground. "Getting their feet under them" for most animals is a matter of what's touching the soles of their feet.

WHAT GOOD IS A FOOT?

This ice climber has strapped crampons onto his boots to provide firm footing, even on a vertical surface.

9.
GETTING DOWN TO THE BOTTOM OF FEET

From an observation point far below, people watch through high-powered glasses as a group of climbers descends the Grand Teton. Up on the mountain, the air is thin and the sun's rays are strong. The climbers' red nylon jackets are vibrant against the rock face.

The climbers inch carefully along a narrow rock-strewn ledge. One stumble and a mountaineer could fly suddenly and unexpectedly into thin air. But the climbers' movements are controlled and sure. They checked their equipment before they set out. They know that the ropes that connect them to each other are in good condition. And they are wearing boots with thick, deeply ribbed soles. The soles of their boots help the climbers move safely up and down the mountain.

People who climb on ice fields or frozen waterfalls alter the bottoms of their feet, too. They strap a crampon onto each foot before they begin. A crampon is a metal plate with strong metal points around the edge of the sole. Two more points stick out on the toe. The points of the crampons drive into ice and give the climbers a foothold.

CRAMPONS

MOUNTAIN
CLIMBING
BOOTS

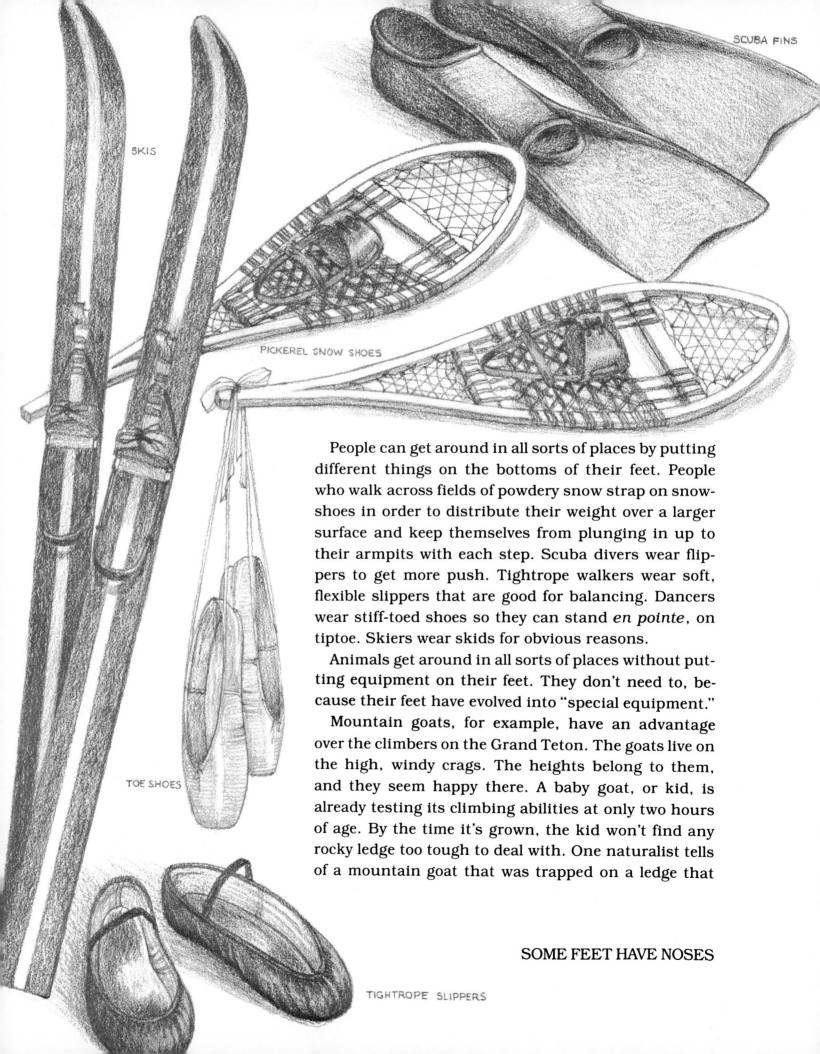

SCUBA FINS

SKIS

PICKEREL SNOW SHOES

TOE SHOES

People can get around in all sorts of places by putting different things on the bottoms of their feet. People who walk across fields of powdery snow strap on snow-shoes in order to distribute their weight over a larger surface and keep themselves from plunging in up to their armpits with each step. Scuba divers wear flippers to get more push. Tightrope walkers wear soft, flexible slippers that are good for balancing. Dancers wear stiff-toed shoes so they can stand *en pointe*, on tiptoe. Skiers wear skids for obvious reasons.

Animals get around in all sorts of places without putting equipment on their feet. They don't need to, because their feet have evolved into "special equipment."

Mountain goats, for example, have an advantage over the climbers on the Grand Teton. The goats live on the high, windy crags. The heights belong to them, and they seem happy there. A baby goat, or kid, is already testing its climbing abilities at only two hours of age. By the time it's grown, the kid won't find any rocky ledge too tough to deal with. One naturalist tells of a mountain goat that was trapped on a ledge that

SOME FEET HAVE NOSES

TIGHTROPE SLIPPERS

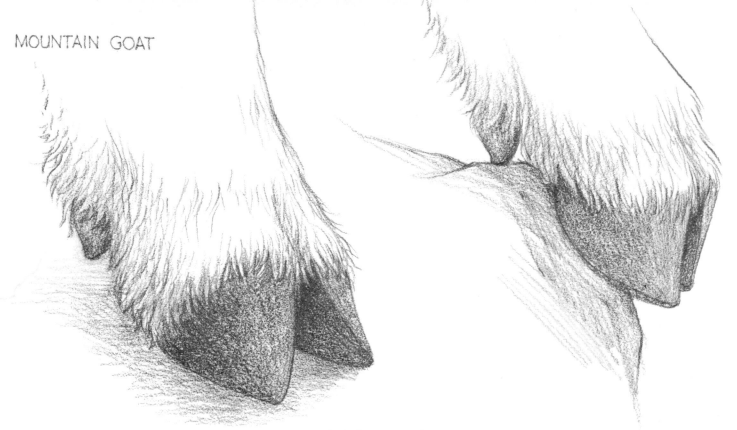

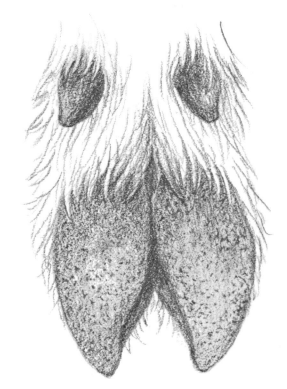

narrowed into nothing. The goat didn't jump down to the next ledge 400 feet below. Instead, it planted its front feet and walked its back end over its head along the sheer rock face. The goat cartwheeled around to face the direction from which it had come!

A mountain goat can do this partly because it has an extremely good sense of balance. It doesn't need ropes to come down a steep rock chute. It just bounces back and forth off the sides. Goats are very strong. Their legs are heavy and muscled and flexible. A goat can stretch its legs out or flex them until its chest is almost touching the ground next to its hooves.

But most important of all, the mountain goat has built-in climbing "boots." The goat's hooves are broad and big. The two toes are flexible and can be spread wide apart. This helps the foot grip a large area. And a goat can draw its toes together, too, in order to grab on to a knob of rock. On the bottom of the goat's toes are rough traction pads. The pads are skid-resistant. On wet or icy rocks, the bottoms of a goat's feet do their stuff to keep the goat safe.

Mountain goats can cling to almost any surface with their remarkable hooves.

GETTING DOWN TO THE BOTTOM OF FEET

Ptarmigans grow "snow-shoes" in the wintertime to keep them from sinking into the snow.

Goats seem to be happiest when jumping from one rock to another, even though one slip could mean falling to their deaths. They find deep snow tougher going, however, and they plow through it at a slow walk. Other animals deal with snow differently. When the winter comes on, they grow "snowshoes"!

The beautiful North American lynx is a cat that grows snowshoes. So do birds such as the willow ptarmigan and the ruffed grouse. Instead of plowing through snow, these animals will move around on top of it. Thick hairs or feathers grow on the bottoms of their feet. This increases the supporting surface of the feet and keeps the animals from sinking in. When summer comes and the snow melts away, the birds and the cat shed their snowshoes.

The northern reindeer also has feet that change for the winter. This reindeer lives in Europe and Asia in the same harsh climate as its American cousin, the caribou. Long, spiny hairs grow on the reindeer's feet,

SOME FEET HAVE NOSES

PTARMIGAN   LYNX   "BEAR PAW" SNOWSHOE

Ptarmigans and lynxes have built-in snowshoes, but humans have to strap on artificial ones.

making them larger. The edges of each foot puff out, and the soft spot in the middle gets smaller. The foot becomes very durable and sharp. In addition to acting like snowshoes, the reindeer's feet can now work like hoes. The animals scrape away snow to get at the moss underneath. This food will keep them from starving during the long, frozen winter.

Some animals have a "watershoe" version of snowshoes on the bottoms of their feet. They take advantage of the surface film, the strong elastic crust of water. Most insects' feet end in claws, but the water strider's feet don't. (They do have claws, but the claws are a little above the tips of the feet.) The water strider's feet end in fanlike tufts of hairs—watershoes! These insects move around on the top of the water, leaving dimples on the surface film instead of footprints.

The water strider's feet work so well that the insect can leap and land on the water again without breaking through. But even if a strider fell through the surface film, it wouldn't sink. It has a coat of fine hairs. The strider traps air in these hairs and buoys itself up with them. The air also keeps the insect dry. Water striders fly well, too. When they fly, they don't need their watershoes, so the hairs fold down against their legs to cut wind resistance.

GETTING DOWN TO THE BOTTOM OF FEET

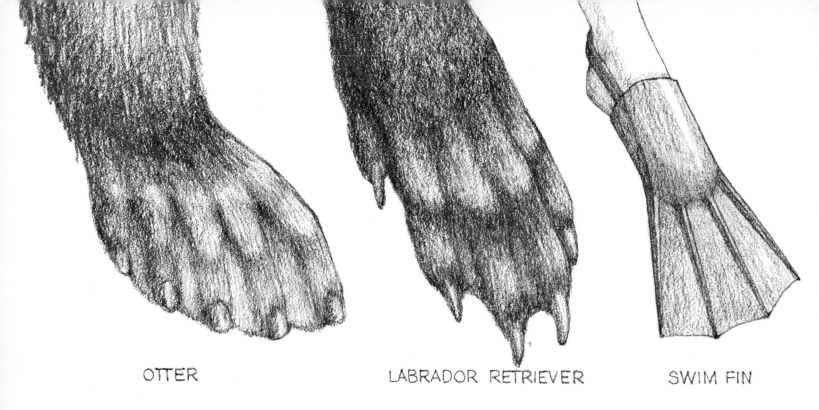

OTTER   LABRADOR RETRIEVER   SWIM FIN

People have to don artificial flippers to compete with otters and Labrador retrievers.

Animals with webs between their toes are well equipped for water. When they paddle, the webbed soles of their feet give them a good push. Ducks and other water birds have webs of different kinds, of course. Otters have large hind feet that are webbed or fringed with stiff hairs. Claws stick out from the otter's webs and are used to catch the crawfish it eats. Otters must love to play in the water, they do it so much. So do Labradors and Viszlas—dogs with webbed feet. These dogs can swim so well that a person tossing sticks into the water for one to bring back will get tired long before the dog wants to stop. Sometimes the dogs even toss the stick for themselves, and fetch it back. And toss it again. And again.

One of the most unusual of the web-footed animals is the Surinam toad. It seldom leaves the muddy streams of South America where it lives. Its flat body is almost square and its head is triangular, with little beady eyes. This toad has star-shaped discs under its front toes and broad webs between its back toes. The Surinam toad may never win a beauty contest, but it swims like a champ.

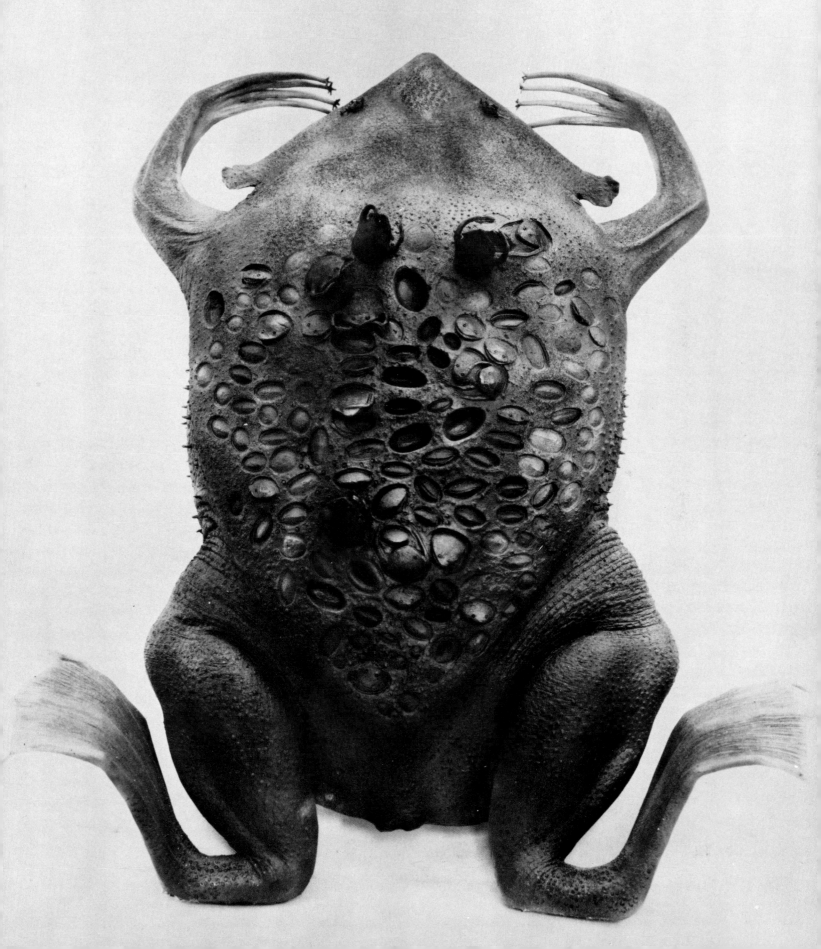

The Surinam toad's webbed feet make it an ace swimmer. This one is in the process of hatching dozens of baby toads from eggs stored on its back.

Still another amphibian uses its webs—not to swim, but to fly. The flying frog lives in the treetops of South America and Asia. It goes after insects by jumping out into the air. A flying frog never seems to look first for a landing place. If a twig or branch doesn't present itself, the frog simply spreads its webbed fingers and toes and glides to the ground on these web-wings.

Walking over desert sands is like walking on water. The tiny grains shift and slide with each step. Yet a camel can trot along carrying 500 pounds or more and never sink in. That's probably why the camel has been called the "ship of the desert."

The camel's feet have evolved to make them useful for desert travel. But even though moving over sand is like moving over water, the camel didn't develop webs. Instead, larger and softer feet appeared over generations. A camel can spread its two toes wide. Its feet are so large that one of them can cover a dinner plate. Size and softness of sole is how the camel's feet meet the challenge of traveling over the sand. Their feet function much like the fat tires of a dune buggy.

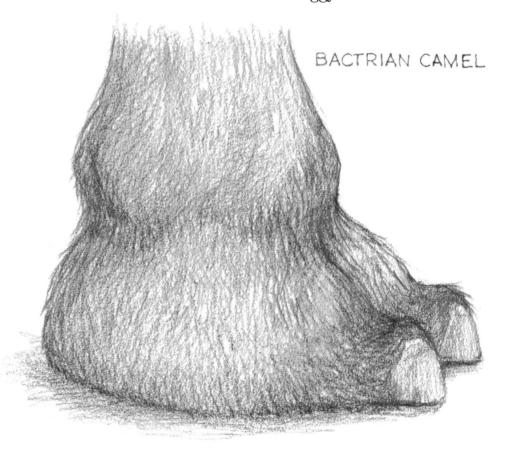

BACTRIAN CAMEL

86

Life on the shimmering deserts is hard. The Sahara Desert can get so hot that falling rain evaporates before it reaches the ground. The sun glares through these phantom rains. The animals that live here must save as much energy as possible when they move, and large flat feet save energy. Even people change when generations of them call the Sahara home. One naturalist finds that the feet of nomadic tribes are bigger and broader than the feet of Europeans. So both people and camels have developed big feet, the kind that work best in the deserts.

The camel's feet are specially adapted to enable it to move smoothly across desert sands.

GETTING DOWN TO THE BOTTOM OF FEET

GECKO'S FOOT

HORIZONTAL PLATES ON ONE TOE

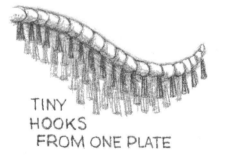

TINY HOOKS FROM ONE PLATE

Smaller desert dwellers, which live among the grains of sand, have developed in other ways. On the bottoms of the feet of these lizards and insects are tiny hooks. The hooks snag roughnesses in the sand to help the animals move efficiently.

Hooks help in other places, too. About 300 species of geckos live all over the world, from sandy deserts to jungles. Geckos are reptiles and their feet are hooked. A gecko can walk across a ceiling or up a smooth pane of glass. Wherever there is anything to walk on, a gecko can walk there. Its toes have pads on their bottoms. The pads have horizontal plates. Each of the plates is covered with many hooked cells. The hooks are tiny, but they catch on to whatever they touch. In addition to these tiny hooks, the gecko's toes end in big hooks—sharp claws. Geckos use these claws to climb trees and on other rough surfaces.

The hooked soles of geckos' feet work so well that many people think geckos have sucker feet. They don't. But most frogs that live in trees do have suckers on the bottoms of their feet. The frogs usually have eight fingers and ten toes. Each of these digits ends in a suction disc. The frogs can climb trees and they can hang upside down on a leaf or even a blade of grass. The tree frogs are so agile that they're like trapeze artists. In fact, if it's taken away from its home in the trees, the barking tree frog will work out on a toy trapeze.

The suction discs work perfectly in a little white frog that lives inside a lily blossom. It may share its lily cup with two or three other little white frogs. The arum frogs are only one inch long, so they fit inside the arum lily nicely. When this frog shoots out of its lily blossom home, one toe may touch a blade of grass. That's enough suction power to hold the arum frog. But if it wants to keep moving, the frog can leap another two feet ahead or another foot and a half up. With only one

SOME FEET HAVE NOSES

sucker, the arum frog can land on a twig, flip around it, and disappear out of sight in a twinkling.

And many insects, too, can walk up or down or upside down with ease. A honeybee has a "glue" foot. Like those of most other insects, a bee's foot ends in a pair of claws. But between these claws is a pad of hollow hairs. If the bee walks on a rough surface, it uses its claws. If the surface is smooth and slick, the bee grabs for another kind of support. Its pad of hairs is automatically snapped open by a tiny clamp. A secretion moistens the hairs, and the moist hairs keep the bee up by "glueing" the feet to the surface. Houseflies also have "glue" feet.

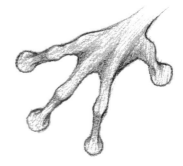

TREE FROG

Jumping spiders are the only spiders that can walk up a smooth surface. If a jumping spider finds itself at the bottom of a deep bathtub, it can walk up and out before the light goes on and it's trapped. They have a "glue" pad of hairs between their claws, too.

For other spiders, the problem is not how to *get* their feet to stick. Their problem is how to *keep* their feet from sticking. Spiders catch their food in webs spun partly of sticky threads. How does a spider get to the fly caught in its web without getting caught itself? The secret is that the bottoms of a spider's feet sweat oil. The oil keeps a spider from getting caught in its own web.

HONEY BEE

Sand and snow, rock and ice, in or on the waters, up and down the walls and trees—each surface calls for different feet. Wherever an animal lives, it lives better with the proper bottoms on its feet. The remarkable changes that appear in the world of feet extend even to the sole.

SPIDER

GETTING DOWN TO THE BOTTOM OF FEET

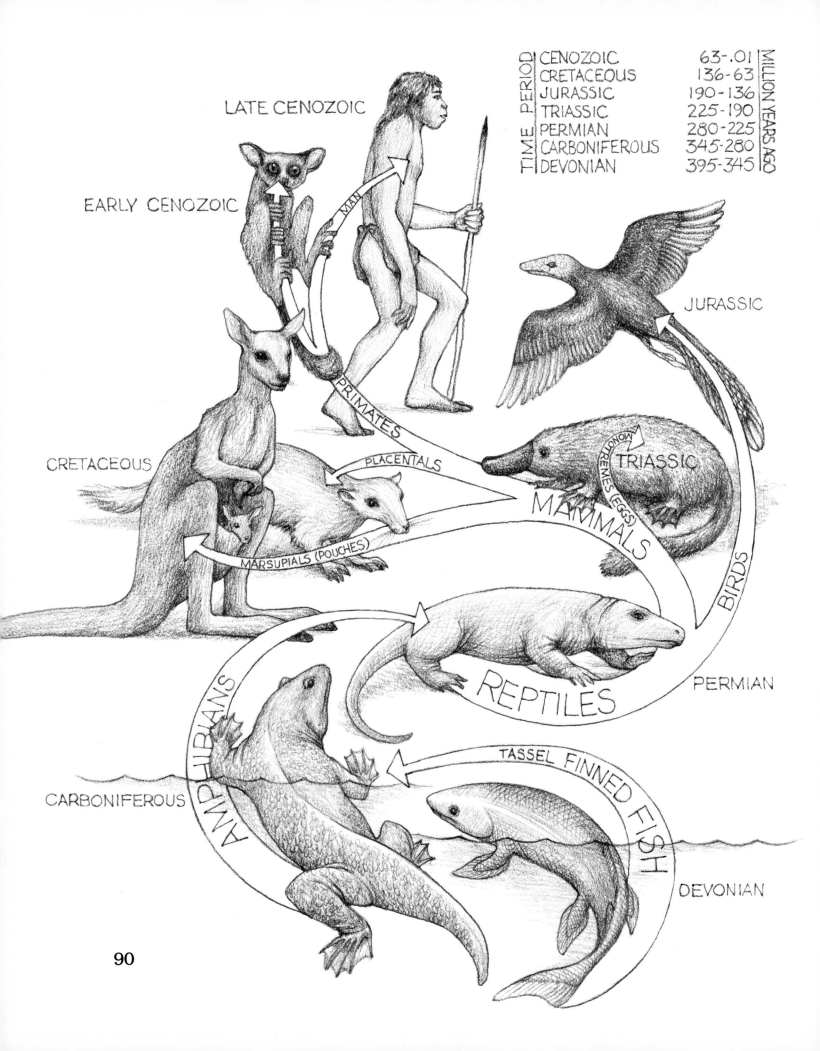

LATE CENOZOIC

EARLY CENOZOIC

CRETACEOUS

CARBONIFEROUS

TIME PERIOD | MILLION YEARS AGO
CENOZOIC   63-.01
CRETACEOUS   136-63
JURASSIC   190-136
TRIASSIC   225-190
PERMIAN   280-225
CARBONIFEROUS   345-280
DEVONIAN   395-345

JURASSIC

MAN

PRIMATES

PLACENTALS

MARSUPIALS (POUCHES)

MONOTREMES (EGGS)

TRIASSIC

MAMMALS

BIRDS

REPTILES

PERMIAN

AMPHIBIANS

TASSEL FINNED FISH

DEVONIAN

90

10.
ANOTHER LOOK AT THE FOOT

Is that all there is to know about feet?

Of course not!

We've barely tickled the surface of the subject of feet.

Consider your own foot again. If you look very closely with a wondering eye, you might see ghosts of the past glimmering around it. Because your foot is the latest step in a long line of feet.

The line started 390 million years ago when the first fishes moved onto land. When these fishes came out of the water for their first short walks, there was no other living creature to greet them. But the waters were full of life, and the first walking fishes returned to live among the mollusks and the spiny-skinned, tube-feet machines.

Many years later, a descendant of these fishes crawled out of the waters. This animal had a long skull and strong shoulder and hip bones. It could breathe with lungs, and it had limbs and feet. It still had a long fish tail, though, and it couldn't leave the water once and for all. This was the first amphibian, and by now there was some life on land—insects.

The first amphibians were looking at a whole new world of food for them when they saw the insects. Best of all, no other creature on land fought with or threatened the newcomers.

More years went by and the amphibians' skins toughened up. They could get farther and farther from the waters because evaporation wasn't such a danger any longer. Their backbones grew stronger and their legs and feet worked better than any that had appeared up to this time. They walked over the swampy land, past tall ferns waving against the sky. There were many shallow, warm seas. Mollusks and starfish tube-feet machines continued to live in the waters. And, above all this, insects now began to fly on wings.

But still, although they were themselves capable of living on dry land, the amphibians went back to the waters to mate and reproduce. And that's the way things remained, until one day one amphibian did something different. It produced an egg with a tough, leathery shell. That was a huge step forward. While all the other amphibians were going back and forth from water to land, while different kinds of frogs and toads and salamanders were evolving, the new breed had made the big step. They were forever free of the waters. The reptiles had appeared.

The oldest fossil eggs ever found were discovered in Texas. They can be dated to about 280 million years ago. And the reptiles were already well advanced at that time. Their lungs were improved and their skin was tough and scaly. The reptiles were ready and the reptiles were able, and the scaly reptiles took over the earth.

Sixty million years would pass before the dinosaurs appeared. During that long unraveling of time, some of the reptiles rose to fly in the air. And some of the reptiles creeping through the swamps began to change in another small way.

Nothing dramatic—no wings, no feathers. The change in the creepers was a small one, but it was one with great meaning. Some of these creeping reptiles grew longer and slimmer leg bones. That's all. Not much to shout about, but these animals, the synapsids, would become the mammals. Longer legs held their bodies off the ground so the animals could move faster, could catch something to chew.

More time ambled by, and now the mammals had appeared. The mammals gave special care to their young. They gave them milk and they gave them protection. So these little mammals had a better chance to survive than most other animals born on the earth.

Then the world changed. It became less kind to reptiles. Now was the mammals' turn to rule. Just as the reptiles had done before them, the mammals exploded in numbers and kinds. Some mammals flourished. Others did not.

One group of mammals found life in the trees safe. These were tiny creatures that caught insects to eat. Their fingers and toes could move and flex, and soon these animals had working hands and working feet. They could smell and hear and their vision was good. Some of these animals remained in the trees and became the monkeys of today.

But others of this group came down to the ground. They stood flatly and firmly upon the earth. The world was dangerous, but with a small change here and an adjustment there, plus enough time—more millions of years—this group of mammals became human beings. From the group that came down from the trees, after a long time, you and I came.

Consider your feet. Any ghosts? Any glimmers? What you're looking at now is the incredible end of the long, long story of the feat of feet! And think about this—with so many changes along the way, who's to say that the story is finished. . . .

BIBLIOGRAPHY

Armstrong, Edward A. *The Life and Lore of the Bird*. N.Y.: Crown Publishers, Inc., 1975.

Austin, Oliver L., Jr. *Birds of the World*. N.Y.: Golden Press, 1961.

Berger, Andrew J. *Bird Study*. N.Y.: Dover Publications, Inc., 1971.

Buchsbaum, Ralph. *Animals Without Backbones*. Rev. ed. Chicago: University of Chicago Press, 1948.

Chadwick, Douglas H. "Mountain Goats: Daring Guardians of the Heights," *National Geographic*, August, 1978, pp. 284-296.

Cirlot, J.E. *A Dictionary of Symbols*. N.Y.: Philosophical Library, 1962.

Cochran, Doris. *Living Amphibians of the World*. Garden City, N.Y.: Doubleday & Company, Inc., 1961.

Crompton, John. *The Life of the Spider*. Boston: Houghton Mifflin Company, 1951.

de Lys, Claudia. *A Treasury of American Superstitions*. N.Y.: Philosophical Library, 1948.

Dillon, Lawrence S. *Animal Variety*. 2nd ed. Dubuque, Iowa: Wm. C. Brown Company Publishers, 1970.

Evans, Ivor H., ed. *Brewer's Dictionary of Phrase & Fable*. N.Y.: Harper & Row, Publishers, 1970.

Farb, Peter. *The Insects*. N.Y.: Time-Life, Inc., 1962.

Frost, S. W. *Insect Life and Insect Natural History*. 2nd rev. ed. N.Y.: Dover Publications, Inc., 1959.

Geist, Valerius. *Mountain Sheep: A Study in Behavior and Evolution*. Chicago: University of Chicago Press, 1971.

George, Uwe. *In the Deserts of This Earth*. N.Y.: Harcourt Brace Jovanovich, 1977.

Kensinger, George. *Strangest Creatures of the World*. N.Y.: Bantam Books, 1977.

Kent, George C., Jr. *Comparative Anatomy of the Vertebrates*. 2nd ed. St. Louis: The C. V. Mosby Company, 1969.

Lagler, Karl F., *et al. Ichthyology*. Ann Arbor, Michigan: University of Michigan Press, 1962.

Larousse Encyclopedia of Animal Life. N.Y.: McGraw-Hill Book Company, 1967.

Linsenmaier, Walter. *Insects of the World*. N.Y.: McGraw-Hill Book Company, 1972.

Marshall, N. B. *The Life of Fishes*. N.Y.: Universe Books, 1966.

Milne, Lorus and Margery. *Invertebrates of North America*. N.Y.: Doubleday & Company, Inc., n.d.

Moore, Ruth. *Evolution*. N.Y.: Time-Life, Inc., 1964.

Naumov, N. P. *The Ecology of Animals*. Chicago: University of Illinois Press, 1972.

Newman, L. H. *Man and Insects: Insect Allies and Enemies*. Garden City, N.Y.: Natural History Press, 1966.

Polunin, Ivan. "Who Says Fish Can't Climb Trees?" *National Geographic*, January, 1972, pp. 85-91.

Schmidt-Nielsen, Knut. *Animal Physiology*. 2nd ed. Englewood Cliffs, N.J.: Prentice-Hall, Inc., 1964.

Scott, John Paul. *Animal Behavior*. Garden City, N.Y.: Doubleday & Company, Inc., 1963.

Skutch, Alexander F. *Parent Birds and Their Young*. Austin: University of Texas Press, 1976.

Wood Gerald L. *Animal Facts & Feats*. N.Y.: Bantam Books, 1978.

INDEX

Entries in *italics* indicate
illustrations

Amphibians, 77, 91-92
Ankles, 8, 9, 51
Apes, *62*, 76
Arachnids, 25, 34
　See also Spiders
Arthropods, 23-25, *24-25*
Arum frog, 88-89
Avocet, *53*

Babies' feet, 8-10, *8, 9, 10*
Bat, *60*, 67
Bear, 62, *62*
Beaver, 71
Bee, 36, 70, *70*, 89, *89*
Binding of feet, 11-13, *11, 12, 13*
Birds
　of prey, 54, *54, 55*
　running, 56-57, *56, 57*
　swimming, 52-53, *52-53*
　toes of, 51-59
　walking, 58, *58, 59*
　See also specific birds
Blenny, 40, *41*
Blue whale, *18*
Boxing, with the feet, 72
Butterfly, *25*, 35, *35*

Camel, 86-87, *86, 87*
Caterpillar, *25*, 77, *77*
Catfish, walking, *38*, 40, *42, 43*
Cat, *17*, 63, 71, *71*, 73, *73*
Centipede, 22-23, 25, *25*, 77
Chimney swift, 54, *54*
Chimpanzee, *62*
China, binding of feet in, 11-13
Clam, 20, *20*, 30-31, *30-31*

Claws
　birds', 51, *51, 52, 53*, 54, *54, 59, 68, 74*
　cats', *71*, 73, *73*
Cleaning, use of feet for, 36, *37, 68*, 70-71, *71*
Climbers, mountain, *78*, 79
Coly, 54, *54*
Coot, American, 53, *53*
Cormorant, *50*, 52-53, *52*
Courser, 56, *56*
Crampon, *78*, 79, *79*

Deer, 66
Desert dwellers, 48-49, 86-88
Dewclaw, 63, *63*, 65, 66
Digitigrade animals, 63
Dog, 63, *63*, 71, 84
Dolphin, 19, 67
Dragonfly, *17*
Duck, 52, *52*, 59, 84

Echinoderms, 27
Elephant, *61*, 64, *64*
Evolution, 19, 63-66, *90*, 91-93

Fin feet, fishes with, 39-48
Fishes, 91
　"walking," *38*, 39-48
　with fin feet, 39-48
　tassel-finned, 39, *39*, 40
Flat feet, animals that walk on, 62
Fly, 36, *36, 37*, 89
Foot binding, 11-13, *11, 12, 13*
Footprints, human, 10, *10*

Frogs
　arum, 88-89
　flying, 86
　sheep, 72
　suction discs on feet of, 88-89
　tree, *6*, 88, *89*

Gecko, 88, *88*
Giraffe, *64*, 65
"Glue" feet, 89, *89*
Goat, 65
　mountain, 66, 80-82, *81*
Gorilla, 76, *76*
Grebe, *53*

Halitherium, *18*
Hands, feet used as, 74, 76
Hawk, 54, *54*
　red-shouldered, *55*
Heron, *68*, 71
Hippopotamus, *64*, 65, *65*
Honeybee, 70, *70*, 89, *89*
Hooves, 64, *64*
　cloven, 64, *64*
　goats', 81, *81*
Horse, 64, *64*, 73
Housefly, 36, *36, 37*, 89
Human feet, 7, 8-13, *8-9, 10, 12, 13, 17*, 51, *62*, 72, *76, 78, 79*-80, *83, 84*, 87
Hummingbird, 58, *59*

Insects, 25, 34, 91, 92
　feet and legs as tools of, 69-71
　See also specific insects

Jacana, 58, *58, 59*

Kangaroo, *16*, 73, 74

Labrador retriever, 84, *84*
Locomotion, methods of, 12, 20, *20*, 22, 25, 29, 39-40, 43, 48, 54, 56, 57, 58, 62, 69, 80-81, 88-89
Lungfish, 40, *41*, *42*, 43
Lynx, 82, *83*

Macaw, *75*
Mammals, 61-67, 92, 93
Millipede, 25, *25*
Mole, 66, *66*
Mole cricket, 71, *71*
Mollusks, 20, *21*
Monkeys, 62, 76, 93
Mousebird, 54
Mudskipper, 44, *45*, 46, *47*, 48

Nereis, 22, *23*
"Noses," feet with, 33-34, *33*, *34*
Number of feet, in different species, 17-25

Ostrich, 56-57, *56*, *57*, 73
Otter, 84, *84*

Paleoparadoxia, *18*
Parrot, 74, *75*
Penguin, *52*
Perch, climbing, *42*, 43-44
Pig, *64*, 65
Plantigrade animals, 62
Porpoise, 19, 67, *67*
Ptarmigan, 82, *82*, *83*

Reindeer, 82-83
Reptiles, 92, 93
Rhinoceros, 64, *64*
Romans, ancient, 15, *15*

Salamander, 69, 77
Sayings about feet, 14
Scorpion, whip, 34, *34*
Sea star, *26*, 27-31, *27*, *28*, *29*, *30-31*
Sheep, 65
    mountain, 66, 71
Sheep frog, 72, *72*
Shovels, feet used as, 66, 71-72
Skate, 40
Skink, 48-49, *48*, *49*
Smell, sense of, 33-36
Snowshoes, 80, *80*, 82, 83, *83*
Soles of feet, *76*, 79-89
Squirrel, *61*, 67, 74
Spadefoot toad, 72
Spider, 25, *32*, 33, 36, *89*
    jumping, 89
Starfish, *26*, 27-31, *27*, *28*, *29*, *30-31*
Suction discs, 88-89
Superstitions about feet, 14-15
Surinam toad, 84, *85*
Swift, chimney, 54, *54*
Swivel toe, 54, *54*

Talons, 54, 59
Tarantula, *33*
Tassel-finned fishes, 39-40, *39*

Taste, sense of, 34-36
Thumb, opposable, 74, 76
Tiptoe, animals that move on, 62, 63
Toads
    spadefoot, 72
    Surinam, 84, *85*
Toenails, animals that move on, 64, 65
Toes
    big, 9, 76
    birds', 51-59
    number of, 62-66
    swivel, 54, *54*
    vestigial, *see* Dewclaws
    webbed, *50*, 52, *52-53*, 53, 59, 84, 86
Tools, feet as, 69-72, *70*, *71*
Traction pads, 81
Tree frog, *6*, 88, *89*

Ungulates, 64

Vertebrates, 39, 71

Water, feet adapted for, 83-84
Water boatman, 69, *69*
Water strider, 83
Weapons, feet as, *16*, 72-73
Webbed feet, *50*, 52, *52-53*, 53, 59, 84, 86
Whale, 19, 67
    blue, *18*
Whip scorpion, 34, *34*
Winter, feet that adapt to, 82-83
Worm snake, 19